Dinner Made Easy
with
six sisters' *stuff*

Dinner Made Easy

with

six sisters' *stuff*

Time-Saving Recipes **for busy moms**

SHADOW
MOUNTAIN

To our amazing fans and readers who
have supported us over the years.

All photographs courtesy SixSistersStuff.com, except the following photographs: shopping list on page 26 © viviamo/Shutterstock.com; refrigerator on page 26 © Ljupco Smokovski/Shutterstock.com; chopping vegetables on page 27 © sinicak/Shutterstock.com; slowcooker on page 27 © Lighttraveler/Shutterstock.com; kitchen shears on page 27 © Marie C Fields/Shutterstock.com; person chopping on page 148 © Dragon Images/Shutterstock.com; eggs on page 148 © Kunertus/Shutterstock.com; pomegranate on page 148 © OZMedia/Shutterstock.com; citrus fruit on page 148 © Evgeny Karandaev/Shutterstock.com; honey on page 149 © Natalia Klenova/Shutterstock.com; onion on page 149 © MaraZe/Shutterstock.com; muffins on page 149 © Dejan Stanic Micko/Shutterstock.com; dishwasher on page 149 © Kunertus/Shutterstock.com.

Library of Congress Cataloging-in-Publication Data
Names: Six Sisters' Stuff, issuing body.
Title: Dinner made easy with Six Sisters' Stuff : time-saving recipes for busy moms / Six Sisters' Stuff.
Description: Salt Lake City, Utah : Shadow Mountain, [2016] | ©2016 | Includes index.
Identifiers: LCCN 2016008703 | ISBN 9781629722283 (paperbound)
Subjects: LCSH: Quick and easy cooking. | Dinners and dining. | LCGFT: Cookbooks.
Classification: LCC TX833.5 .D545 2016 | DDC 641.5/12—dc23
LC record available at http://lccn.loc.gov/2016008703

Printed in China
Global Interprint, Inc., Shenzhen, China

10 9 8 7 6 5 4 3 2 1

CONTENTS

A Six Sisters' Secret: To help make your dinner planning even easier, we've identified some recipes that fall into one or more categories by using the following icons:

 30 MINUTES OR LESS   **5 INGREDIENTS OR LESS**

 PANTRY FAVORITES   **SLOW COOKER MEALS**

 FREEZER MEALS   **ONE PAN, ONE POT MEALS**

 CASSEROLES

Watch for them throughout the cookbook, and happy cooking!

On those nights that are particularly hectic, try one of the recipes in this section. Each recipe is filling, delicious, and can be thrown together in 20 to 30 minutes. Many double for great lunch ideas as well.

30 MINUTES OR LESS

Chicken Cordon Bleu French Bread Pizza

Prep time: 10 minutes | Cook time: 10 minutes | Total time: 20 minutes | Serves: 8

1 loaf French bread

1 (16-ounce) jar Alfredo sauce, or 2 cups homemade Alfredo sauce

1 teaspoon garlic salt

1 teaspoon Italian seasoning

4 cups shredded mozzarella cheese

1 cup shredded swiss cheese

2 cups cooked, diced breaded chicken, such as Tyson Crispy Chicken Strips

½ cup diced cooked ham

¼ cup bacon bits

4 to 5 green onions, thinly sliced

Preheat oven to 400 degrees F.

Cut loaf of French bread in half lengthwise and place cut sides up on a large baking sheet. Spread Alfredo sauce evenly over bread, using as much or as little as you like. Sprinkle garlic salt and Italian seasoning on top of sauce.

Top with mozzarella cheese, swiss cheese, cooked chicken, ham, bacon bits, and green onions. Bake 10 minutes, or until cheese starts to melt.

Cut into slices and serve.

Quick Prep Tip: Use pre-cooked bacon (such as Oscar Mayer Real Bacon Bits) and packaged ham (such as Oscar Mayer Carving Board Ham).

Turkey Cranberry Wrap

Prep time: 15 minutes | Total time: 15 minutes | Serves: 4

- 4 spinach tortillas
- 4 tablespoons plain Greek yogurt
- 1 cup spinach leaves
- ½ cup dried cranberries
- ½ medium Granny Smith apple, diced
- ½ cup chopped cooked turkey
- 4 tablespoons crumbled feta cheese

Spread 1 tablespoon Greek yogurt on each tortilla.

Evenly top each tortilla with spinach leaves, dried cranberries, apples, turkey, and feta cheese. Roll up tightly and serve.

Parmesan Pork Chops

Prep time: 10 minutes │ Cook time: 16 minutes │ Total time: 26 minutes │ Serves: 4

4	boneless pork chops	1	teaspoon seasoned salt
½	cup Italian seasoned bread crumbs		Salt and pepper to taste
½	cup grated Parmesan cheese	¼	cup milk

Preheat oven to 375 degrees F. Coat a 9x9-inch pan with cooking spray.

In a small bowl, mix together bread crumbs, cheese, seasoned salt, and salt and pepper.

Pour milk into a separate, shallow bowl.

Dredge each pork chop in the milk and then the crumb mixture, making sure each is completely coated.

Place the pork chops in the prepared pan and bake 8 to 10 minutes on each side.

Serving Suggestion: For a weekend meal or on an evening when you have more time to cook, try these pork chops served over mashed potatoes and drizzled with gravy made from the juices in the pan.

Skillet Pork Lo Mein ⑤

Prep time: 10 minutes | Cook time: 10 minutes | Total time: 20 minutes | Serves: 6

- 8 ounces uncooked angel hair pasta
- 1 (1-pound) pork tenderloin
- 1 (16-ounce) bag frozen stir fry vegetables
- 1 cup teriyaki sauce
- ¼ teaspoon ground ginger

Cook pasta as directed on package. Drain water and cover to keep warm. While the pasta is cooking, cut the pork tenderloin in half lengthwise, then cut crosswise into ¼-inch-thick slices. Heat a large, nonstick skillet over medium-high heat. Add pork and cook 3 minutes, stirring frequently. Stir in the frozen vegetables, teriyaki sauce, and ginger. Continue to cook until it starts to boil, then reduce heat to medium-low, cover, and simmer 3 to 5 minutes (or until the pork is no longer pink and vegetables are tender). Stir in the cooked pasta and gently mix until the noodles are coated in the sauce. Heat through and serve.

> **Serving Suggestion:** Substitute spaghetti noodles for angel hair pasta.

Taco Salad Casserole

Prep time: 5 minutes | Cook time: 14 minutes | Total time: 19 minutes | Serves: 6

1 pound ground beef or turkey

¼ cup diced onion

¼ cup diced green pepper

1 cup crushed tortilla chips

1 (16-ounce) can refried beans

½ cup water

1 (1-ounce) packet taco seasoning or 2 tablespoons Homemade Taco Seasoning (see recipe on page 103)

1 cup shredded cheddar cheese

Salad toppings, such as shredded lettuce, diced tomatoes, olives, sour cream, etc.

Preheat oven broiler to high. In a large skillet, cook beef, onion, and green pepper over medium heat, stirring occasionally, until meat is browned. While the meat is browning, spread crushed tortilla chips in the bottom of a greased, broiler-safe 8x8-inch pan. Heat the refried beans in a small, microwave-safe bowl for 60 seconds, or until warmed through. Spread the refried beans gently over the top of the tortilla chips. Once the meat is browned, drain and return to stove. Add ½ cup water and taco seasoning and stir until well combined. Pour browned meat mixture over the top of the refried beans. Top with cheddar cheese and place under broiler 2 to 4 minutes, until the cheese is melted and starts to bubble. Top with your favorite salad toppings and serve warm.

Chicken Mushroom Pizza

Prep time: 5 minutes | Cook time: 10 minutes | Total time: 15 minutes | Serves: 6

1 (12-inch) purchased Italian pizza crust

½ cup ranch salad dressing

2 teaspoons minced garlic

1 cup chopped cooked chicken (about ½ pound boneless, skinless chicken breast halves)

1 (4-ounce) can sliced mushrooms

2 cups shredded mozzarella cheese

Preheat oven to 400 degrees F.

Place the pizza crust on a pizza stone or baking sheet. Spread ranch dressing over the top of the crust and then sprinkle evenly with minced garlic. Top with chicken and mushrooms, followed by shredded mozzarella cheese.

Bake 10 to 12 minutes, until cheese is melted and the edges start to brown.

Mustard-Apricot Pork Chops

Prep time: 10 minutes | Cook time: 10 minutes | Total time: 20 minutes | Serves: 4

⅓ cup apricot preserves

2 tablespoons Dijon mustard

1 teaspoon soy sauce

3 green onions, chopped

½ teaspoon garlic salt

4 (6-ounce) pork chops

Heat grill to medium heat. In a small saucepan over medium heat, combine preserves, mustard, soy sauce, and onions until preserves are melted and all ingredients are well combined. Rub each pork chop with garlic salt and place on grill. Cook 4 to 5 minutes on each side or until tender and no longer pink. During the last few minutes of grilling, brush some of the apricot glaze over each side of the pork chop, and use the rest to serve on top of the pork.

Loaded Baked Nachos

Prep time: 10 minutes | Cook time: 5 minutes | Total time: 15 minutes | Serves: 10

6 cups tortilla chips

1 pound ground beef

1 (1-ounce) packet taco seasoning or 2 tablespoons Homemade Taco Seasoning (see recipe on page 103)

1 (15-ounce) can black beans, drained and rinsed

2 cups shredded cheddar cheese

2 tomatoes, diced

2 avocados, diced

4 green onions, diced

Salsa

Sour cream

Preheat oven to 350 degrees F. Spread tortilla chips over the bottom of a large baking sheet, making sure to cover the entire surface; set aside.

In a large skillet over medium heat, brown meat until cooked through. Stir in taco seasoning. Spread meat evenly over chips, followed by black beans. Sprinkle cheese over the top and place in oven 5 to 7 minutes, until cheese is melted.

Remove from the oven top with tomatoes, avocados, and green onions, spreading them out as evenly as possible. Serve with salsa and sour cream.

> **Quick Prep Tip:** In a big hurry for dinner? Mix taco seasoning with two cans drained and rinsed black beans and omit the ground beef.

Szechwan Shrimp

Prep time: 5 minutes | Cook time: 15 minutes | Total time: 20 minutes | Serves: 4

4 tablespoons water

2 tablespoons ketchup

1 tablespoon soy sauce

2 teaspoons cornstarch

1 teaspoon honey

½ teaspoon crushed red pepper (optional)

¼ teaspoon ground ginger

1 tablespoon vegetable oil

6 green onions, diced

4 cloves garlic, minced

12 ounces cooked shrimp

2 cups cooked rice

In a medium bowl, stir together water, ketchup, soy sauce, cornstarch, honey, crushed red pepper, if using, and ground ginger; set aside. Heat oil in a large skillet over medium-high heat. Stir in green onions and garlic and cook 1 minute. Add shrimp and stir to coat with seasoned oil. Add sauce and cook and stir until bubbly and thickened. Serve over cooked rice.

Serving Suggestion: If you are looking to make this dish a little healthier, serve it on top of cooked quinoa instead of rice. It is delicious!

Brown Sugar Honey Salmon

Prep time: 5 minutes | Cook time: 15 minutes | Total time: 20 minutes | Serves: 4

- 1 pound salmon filets
- ¼ cup packed brown sugar, plus more for topping
- 1 tablespoon honey
- ½ cup reduced sodium soy sauce
- ¼ cup fresh pineapple juice
- 1 teaspoon Dijon mustard
- 1 teaspoon sesame oil
- 1 tablespoon olive oil
- 1 teaspoon freshly grated ginger
- 2 cloves garlic, finely minced
- 1 teaspoon red chili pepper flakes (optional)

Preheat oven to 400 degrees F. Coat a 9x9-inch baking dish with nonstick cooking spray and line with foil. Spray foil with nonstick cooking spray. Place salmon, skin side down, in pan and set aside.

In a large bowl, whisk together the brown sugar, honey, soy sauce, pineapple juice, mustard, sesame oil, olive oil, ginger, garlic, and red pepper flakes, if using. Brush marinade over salmon. Sprinkle with a little bit of extra brown sugar so the top will caramelize.

Bake 15 to 20 minutes, or until salmon easily flakes with fork.

A Six Sisters' Secret: For a tip on cooking with honey, see Cooking Hack #8 on page 149.

Serving Suggestion: Serve with a side salad for extra flavor.

Caesar Salad Burgers

Prep time: 10 minutes | Cook time: 6 minutes | Total time: 16 minutes | Serves: 4

1 pound ground beef or turkey

1 cup shredded Parmesan cheese, divided

1 teaspoon garlic salt

Chopped romaine lettuce

4 tablespoons Caesar salad dressing

4 hamburger buns

Heat grill to high.

In a large bowl, mix together ground beef or turkey, ½ cup of the Parmesan cheese, and garlic salt. Shape into four ¼-pound patties. Grill for about 3 to 5 minutes on each side.

Top each burger with romaine lettuce, salad dressing, and Parmesan cheese to taste. Serve hot.

Mini Spinach Calzones

Prep time: 10 minutes | Cook time: 10 minutes | Total time: 20 minutes | Serves: 4 to 5

1 package refrigerated pizza dough (or enough dough for 1 pizza)

½ (10-ounce) package frozen chopped spinach, thawed and thoroughly drained

4 ounces cream cheese, softened

3 tablespoons grated Parmesan cheese, divided

2 tablespoons chopped green onion

¼ teaspoon black pepper

¼ teaspoon garlic powder

1 egg white

Preheat oven to 400 degrees F. Spray two baking sheets with nonstick cooking spray.

Spray nonstick cooking spray onto a clean surface and roll out pizza dough into a 15-inch square. Using a pizza cutter or sharp knife, cut pizza dough into 25 3-inch squares.

In a mixing bowl, combine spinach, cream cheese, 2 tablespoons Parmesan cheese, green onion, pepper, and garlic powder.

Spoon a teaspoon of spinach filling in the middle of each square and fold over into a triangle. Use a fork to crimp the edges of the triangle and seal closed.

Place mini calzones onto prepared baking sheets. Brush egg white on the top of each mini calzone and sprinkle with remaining Parmesan cheese.

Bake 10 minutes, or until crust is golden brown.

Lemon Butter Chicken Skillet

Prep time: 5 minutes | Cook time: 10 minutes | Total time: 15 minutes | Serves: 6

6 chicken breast halves, sliced thin

½ cup flour

½ teaspoon salt

⅓ cup butter

Lemon pepper seasoning to taste

2 lemons, sliced about ¼-inch thick

2 tablespoons lemon juice

In a small bowl, mix together flour and salt. Heat butter in a large skillet over medium-high heat. Dredge chicken breasts in flour and sprinkle each with lemon pepper seasoning, then add to the melted butter in the skillet. Cook 2 to 3 minutes on each side, until the chicken starts to brown. Remove from heat and set aside. To the heated butter, add sliced lemons and cook 2 minutes on each side, until lemons start to brown. Add the chicken back to the skillet and drizzle with lemon juice, cooking for about 2 more minutes. Serve warm.

A Six Sisters' Secret: For a tip on juicing fresh lemons, see Cooking Hack #6 on page 148.

Pecan-Crusted Tilapia

Prep time: 15 minutes | Cook time: 5 minutes | Total time: 20 minutes | Serves: 4

1 cup bread crumbs

½ cup finely chopped pecans

¼ teaspoon salt

⅛ teaspoon pepper

3 eggs

3 tablespoons olive oil

4 tilapia fillets

Combine bread crumbs, pecans, salt, and pepper in a shallow bowl. In a separate bowl, beat 3 eggs. Heat oil in a skillet over medium heat. Dredge each tilapia fillet in the egg mixture, then in the pecan and bread crumb mixture, completely coating the fillets. Reduce stovetop temperature to low and add fillets to pan. Fry fillets 2 minutes on each side, or until fish is cooked through and flakes easily with a fork.

A Six Sisters' Secret: For a cooking hack on how to preserve the shelf life of shelled nuts, see Cooking Hack #9 on page 149.

Ham and Pineapple Pizza Roll Ups

Prep time: 15 minutes | Cook time: 15 minutes | Total time: 30 minutes | Serves: 8

- 1 (13.8-ounce) package refrigerated pizza dough
- 1 cup marinara sauce, plus more for serving
- 1 cup cubed cooked ham
- 1 cup pineapple chunks, fresh or canned
- 1 cup shredded cheddar cheese
- 1 cup shredded mozzarella cheese
- Italian seasoning to taste
- Garlic salt to taste

Preheat oven to 350 degrees F. Line a 15x10x1-inch baking sheet with aluminum foil and spray with nonstick cooking spray.

Spread pizza dough out on the baking sheet and then spread the marinara sauce over the dough. Top with cheese, ham, pineapple, and seasonings.

Roll up the dough jelly roll style. Use a sharp knife to cut the roll into 1-inch slices. Arrange cut rolls back on prepared pan and bake 15 to 20 minutes, or until the rolls are golden and the dough is fully cooked.

Serve with marinara sauce for dipping.

> **A Six Sisters' Secret:** An easy and delicious meal that your children can help you whip up in a matter of minutes! Have your picky eaters add their favorite toppings so that it's a meal they are sure to enjoy.

KITCHEN SHORTCUTS AND TIME-SAVERS

Here are some of our favorite shortcuts and tips to make the time you spend in the kitchen stress free and more efficient!

Plan ahead. Plan out all of your meals for the week and write a grocery list to get all the ingredients you'll need. You'll save time and money by only going to the grocery store once a week.

Keep an updated grocery list. As you run out of key ingredients or kitchen staples, keep a list so you can buy them on your next trip to the grocery store. This will keep your pantry and kitchen fully stocked so you'll avoid emergency trips to the store and be ready to cook.

Have a well-stocked freezer. Keep prepared side dishes and vegetables in your freezer that you can easily heat up and serve alongside a main dish.

Organize for convenience. Organize your pantry, fridge, and freezer so you know where everything is. Dinner prep will be quick and smooth if you don't have to search for a key ingredient.

Clean before you cook. Clean off kitchen counters, empty the dishwasher, and get out all of the ingredients you need. This will help dinner preparation—and cleanup—go a lot faster.

Double your recipes. If you know you have a busy week ahead, double a recipe and freeze half to warm up on another night.

Prep food in advance. If you are chopping up vegetables for dinner one evening and know you'll need more later in the week, chop everything all at once and store the extra in an airtight container in the fridge. If you're cutting up fresh fruit or vegetables for snacks or lunches, do it all at once and store in the fridge so they are ready to go when you need them.

Use your slow cooker. Slow cookers are one of the easiest ways to prepare delicious food with very little effort. If you know that you won't have a lot of time to cook dinner in the evening, put a slow cooker recipe in your slow cooker in the morning and have a meal ready at dinnertime.

Try freezer meals. Look for family-friendly freezer meals that you can prepare ahead of time and heat up at dinnertime. Freezer meals are perfect for those nights when you don't have time to cook and help you to avoid eating out.

Buy rotisserie chicken. Many dinner recipes call for cooked or shredded chicken. Cut down on cook time by using a rotisserie chicken. You can get 3 to 4 cups of shredded chicken from one rotisserie chicken.

Use kitchen shears. Kitchen shears make cutting fresh herbs, doughs, and other ingredients much easier than using knives.

Cook big batches. When you are cooking rice, sauces, or soup, make large batches and freeze them in smaller individual bags. They are easy to reheat when you are in a hurry.

Use a pizza cutter. Having kids means always cutting their food into smaller bites. Using a pizza cutter often works better than a knife for cutting food into bite-sized pieces. We use a pizza cutter to cut sandwiches, quesadillas, pancakes, and more!

Make mixes ahead of time. Combine dry ingredients for pancakes, cookies, or muffins and store in resealable plastic bags. Write the recipe on the front in permanent marker.

Sometimes, just looking at a long ingredients list can be enough to stop you from cooking for the night. When you don't want to fuss with lots of ingredients, try one of the meals in this section. They all call for 5 or fewer ingredients but still taste and look great at the table.

5 INGREDIENTS OR LESS

Sweet and Tangy Meatballs

Prep time: 5 minutes │ Cook time: 2 hours │ Total time: 2 hours 5 minutes │ Serves: 8

1 (12-ounce) jar chili sauce

1 (16- to 18-ounce) jar grape jelly

1 (2-pound) package frozen meatballs

4 cups cooked rice (optional)

Spray slow cooker with nonstick cooking spray. Combine chili sauce and jelly in a slow cooker and stir until smooth. Add meatballs and cook on low for 2 to 5 hours.

Serve over rice or with toothpicks.

> **A Six Sisters' Secret:** To make this a quick and easy freezer meal: In a bowl, combine chili sauce and grape jelly until smooth. Place meatballs in a zip-top gallon-sized freezer bag. Pour in the chili sauce mixture and mix together in the bag until thoroughly combined. Zip bag closed and freeze. When ready to eat, remove from freezer and thaw in fridge overnight. Coat slow cooker with nonstick cooking spray and place contents of bag inside slow cooker. Cook on high 1 to 2 hours or low 3 to 4 hours.
>
> **Serving Suggestion:** This dish also makes a great appetizer! You can use regular or turkey meatballs.

Pizza Quesadillas

Prep time: 5 minutes | Cook time: 25 minutes | Total time: 30 minutes | Serves: 4

6 ounces sliced pepperoni	1 (16-ounce) jar pizza sauce
8 (4-inch) tortillas	1 cup shredded mozzarella cheese

Heat skillet over medium heat, add pepperoni slices, and fry until crisp, stirring often; transfer to a paper towel to drain off fat.

Brush each tortilla with a very thin layer of pizza sauce. Sprinkle cheese on top of the sauce on half the tortillas. Top cheese with crisped pepperoni and then sprinkle on another layer of cheese. Place the remaining tortillas, sauce side down, on top of the layered tortillas.

Preheat a greased or nonstick skillet over medium heat. Gently place quesadillas in the pan and cook 3 to 5 minutes on each side, until cheese is melted and tortillas are crispy. Slice into quarters and serve with remaining pizza sauce that has been warmed in the microwave.

Slow Cooker Italian Beef Sandwiches

Prep time: 10 minutes | Cook time: 10 hours | Total time: 10 hours 10 minutes | Serves: 6 to 8

1 (3-pound) bottom round beef roast

1 cup water

2 packets dry Italian salad dressing mix

1 (16-ounce) jar pepperoncini peppers (can substitute milder, sweeter peppers if desired)

6 to 8 hoagie buns, toasted

Place roast in slow cooker. Add water and Italian salad dressing mix. Cook on low 10 to 12 hours. About 2 to 3 hours before serving, take two forks and gently pull apart the beef roast. It should be tender enough to shred easily. Add peppers, including the liquid, to the slow cooker, mix well, and continue cooking on low until ready to serve. Serve on toasted hoagie buns.

Serving Suggestion: To toast buns, split each roll in half and place, cut side up, on a large baking sheet. Butter the top of each half and place under heated broiler 1 to 2 minutes.

Easy Gnocchi Casserole

Prep time: 10 minutes | Cook time: 35 minutes | Total time: 45 minutes | Serves: Serves 4 to 6

1 pound ground Italian sausage

1 (16-ounce) package gnocchi, prepared according to package directions

1 (26-ounce) jar pasta sauce

2 teaspoons Italian seasoning

2 cups shredded mozzarella cheese, divided

Preheat oven to 350 degrees F. Coat a 9x13-inch baking dish with nonstick cooking spray.

In a large skillet over medium heat, brown Italian sausage until cooked through. Drain off fat. Transfer sausage to a large bowl and add prepared gnocchi, pasta sauce, Italian seasoning, and 1 cup of the mozzarella cheese and gently combine.

Spread evenly in prepared pan and bake 25 minutes. Sprinkle remaining cheese on top and cook an additional 10 minutes or until cheese is melted.

> **A Six Sisters' Secret:** Pasta sauce and Italian seasoning are two pantry essentials. For a full list of basic ingredients to keep on hand, see page 47.

Hometown Honey Chipotle Chicken Wings

Prep time: 2 hours 5 minutes | Cook time: 32 minutes | Total time: 2 hours 37 minutes | Serves: 4

1 cup honey	2 teaspoons lime zest
1 cup Tabasco Chipotle sauce	12 to 15 frozen chicken wings, thawed
2 tablespoons fresh lime juice	

In small saucepan, mix together the honey, Tabasco sauce, lime juice, and lime zest over medium heat. Bring to a boil and let simmer 5 minutes. Remove from heat and let mixture cool.

When cool, pour half the mixture into a large zip-top bag, reserving the other half of the sauce for later. Add the chicken wings to the zip-top bag and shake until all the wings are covered in sauce. Refrigerate at least 2 hours or overnight.

When ready to bake, preheat oven to 375 degrees F. Line a baking sheet with aluminum foil and coat with nonstick cooking spray.

Remove wings from bag and place on prepared baking sheet. Bake 30 minutes. Remove from oven. Turn the oven to broil.

With half the remaining sauce, baste the chicken wings and return to the oven. Broil for 1 minute.

Remove the wings and baste again with the rest of the sauce. Broil again for 1 minute. Serve hot.

Club Chicken

Prep time: 10 minutes | Cook time: 1 hour | Total time: 1 hour 10 minutes | Serves: 4

1 cup finely crushed Club or Townhouse brand crackers

1 packet Italian salad dressing mix

2 pounds boneless, skinless chicken breast halves or tenders

3 tablespoons butter, melted

Preheat oven to 375 degrees F. Coat a 9x13-inch baking pan with nonstick cooking spray. Combine cracker crumbs and salad dressing mix in a large zip-top bag. Add chicken 2 pieces at a time and shake in crumb mixture to coat. Place crumb-covered chicken in prepared baking pan. Drizzle chicken with melted butter. Bake 1 hour.

Taco Braid

Prep time: 20 minutes | Cook time: 20 minutes | Total time: 40 minutes | Serves: 6

1   pound ground beef

1   (1-ounce) packet taco seasoning or 2 tablespoons Homemade Taco Seasoning (see recipe on page 103)

1   (13.8-ounce) package refrigerated pizza dough

1   (15-ounce) can refried beans

2   cups shredded cheddar cheese

Preheat oven to 375 degrees F. Lightly grease a baking sheet.

Brown ground beef over medium-high heat in a large skillet. Drain off fat, and then add in taco seasoning and water according to package directions. Set aside.

Shape dough into a large rectangle on the prepared baking sheet. Use a pizza cutter to make ten 1½-inch horizontal cuts along each side of the dough.

Spread the refried beans down the center of the dough, then top with the meat mixture and sprinkle with cheddar cheese. Fold the strips on each side inward to make a braid over the filling.

Bake 20 minutes, until golden brown. Cool 1 to 2 minutes, and then slice and serve.

Meatball Subs

Prep time: 5 minutes │ Cook time: 15 minutes │ Total time: 20 minutes │ Serves: 4

24 frozen meatballs

1 (24-ounce) jar spaghetti sauce

1 cup shredded mozzarella cheese
(can also use sliced mozzarella or
provolone)

4 submarine rolls

Fresh basil for garnish (optional)

Prepare meatballs according to package directions. In a large pan, heat spaghetti sauce over medium heat until warm. Stir in cooked meatballs and let them simmer until heated through. Place 6 meatballs, with sauce, on each open roll and sprinkle with ¼ cup cheese and basil, if using. Place subs on a baking sheet and broil 2 to 3 minutes, until the cheese is melted and the bread starts to turn golden. Serve warm.

Quick Prep Tip: Precooked frozen meatballs are a huge timesaver. Looking for more meatball recipes? Check out page 31!

Green Chile Enchilada Casserole

Prep time: 15 minutes | Cook time: 45 minutes | Total time: 1 hour | Serves: 6 to 8

1 (28-ounce) can green chile enchilada sauce, divided

9 (10-inch) flour tortillas

4 cups shredded cooked chicken (about 2 pounds boneless, skinless chicken breast halves)

2 cups shredded Monterey Jack cheese, divided

1 cup sour cream, divided

Preheat oven to 350 degrees F. Lightly grease an 8x11-inch baking dish.

Spread one-fourth of the enchilada sauce into the baking dish.

Rip up 3 tortillas and layer on top of the enchilada sauce. Top with 2 cups of the shredded chicken, ⅔ cup of the cheese, ½ cup sour cream, and another one-fourth of the enchilada sauce. Repeat.

Top with last 3 torn tortillas, remaining enchilada sauce, and the last ⅔ cup of cheese. Cover and bake 45 minutes. Serve warm.

Ravioli Casserole

Prep time: 10 minutes | Cook time: 30 minutes | Total time: 40 minutes | Serves: 9

- 3½ cups pasta sauce, divided
- 1 (25-ounce) package frozen cheese ravioli, divided
- 2 cups cottage cheese, divided
- 4 cups shredded mozzarella cheese, divided
- ½ cup grated Parmesan cheese

Preheat oven to 350 degrees F. Spread 1 cup pasta sauce in ungreased 9x13-inch pan. Arrange half of the frozen ravioli over pasta sauce, covering the bottom of the pan. Top with half of the remaining pasta sauce, ½ cup cottage cheese, and 1 cup shredded mozzarella cheese. Repeat layers, beginning with ravioli. Top with Parmesan cheese. Bake 30 to 40 minutes, or until cheese begins to bubble.

Marinated Pork Loin

Prep time: 5 minutes | Cook time: Varies depending on grill type; approx. 30 minutes | Total time: Varies | Serves: 6 to 8

1 (2- to 4-pound) whole pork tenderloin
1 (16-ounce) bottle Italian dressing

Put the whole pork loin in an airtight container and cover completely with 1 ½ cups of Italian dressing. Set aside remaining dressing. Let pork marinate in refrigerator overnight. When ready to cook, prep grill. If using a propane or indoor grill, set temperature to the lowest setting. Brush cooking grate with vegetable oil.

If using a charcoal grill, light coals in a chimney starter until charcoal is ashy and white, about 30 minutes. Dump coals onto grill grate and arrange with tongs to create one area of the grill that will be significantly lower in temperature than the other areas. (You want the pork to cook slowly, so it's best to place it on a hot grate but not over direct, intense heat.) Place cooking grate on top, cover with grill lid, and let heat 5 to 10 minutes. Brush cooking grate with vegetable oil just before placing pork on grill.

Set the whole pork loin directly on the grill (place on grill over area with fewer coals if using a charcoal grill) and use tongs to slowly turn it and sear on grill marks. If using a gas grill, after a few minutes, cut the loin into 1-inch slices. Baste each slice with the marinade using the reserved Italian dressing and flip the slices every three minutes or so, basting with marinade each time you do. If using a charcoal grill, baste and turn whole loin every few minutes, keeping the grill covered with lid when not basting. Cook until temperature reaches 145 degrees F. on a meat thermometer. Time will vary depending on what type of grill is used.

Baked Sloppy Joes

Prep time: 20 minutes | Cook time: 13 minutes | Total time: 33 minutes | Serves: 8

1 pound ground turkey

1 medium onion, diced

1 (15.5-ounce) can Manwich Sloppy Joe Sauce

2 packages big-sized refrigerated biscuits

Shredded mozzarella cheese

Preheat oven to 350 degrees F.

In a large skillet over medium-high heat, brown turkey and onions until meat is cooked. Add Manwich sauce and stir until mixture is heated through.

Flatten out each biscuit to make a 4- to 5-inch circle. Add 2 spoonfuls of the turkey mixture to one side of the biscuit. Top meat with some cheese and then fold the biscuit over and pinch it closed. Place filled biscuits on an ungreased baking sheet and bake 13 to 15 minutes, until they are browned on top.

SIX SISTERS' PANTRY STAPLES

We like to create recipes with foods that are already in your pantry so you don't have to go out and buy a huge list of ingredients every time you cook. This is a list of the most common foods found in our own pantries. It may not be the same for everyone, but these are some of the items we just can't live without.

BAKING INGREDIENTS

All-purpose flour
Baking powder
Baking soda
Brown sugar
Cake mix
Chocolate chips
Cocoa powder
Cooking spray
Evaporated milk
Granulated sugar
Oats
Peanut butter
Powdered sugar
Sweetened condensed milk
Wheat flour
Vanilla extract
Yeast

SPICES

Basil
Black pepper
Chili powder
Cinnamon
Cumin
Curry
Garlic salt
Italian seasoning
Nutmeg
Onion powder
Oregano
Parsley
Sage
Salt

COOKING INGREDIENTS

Beef broth
Bread crumbs
Canned black beans
Canned chicken
Canned chili
Canned corn
Canned mandarin oranges
Canned pineapple chunks
Canned tuna
Chicken broth
Cream of chicken soup
Cream of mushroom soup
Honey
Jam
Jell-O
Maple syrup
Noodles
Onion soup mix
Pasta

Ranch dressing packets
Rice
Salad dressing (Italian is our favorite because you can also use it as a marinade)
Salsa
Taco seasoning packets
Tomato paste
Vinegar

OILS/SAUCES

Canola oil
Extra virgin olive oil
Vegetable oil
Pasta sauce
Tomato sauce
BBQ sauce
Ketchup
Soy sauce

A well-stocked pantry and freezer mean you'll always have ingredients on hand to pull together a great meal. Staples such as condensed soups; herbs and spices; frozen veggies; frozen chicken breasts, thighs, and wings; soy sauce, ketchup, and other condiments; canned tomatoes and sauce; dried pasta and sauce; crackers; and so on should always be part of a well-stocked kitchen.

PANTRY FAVORITES

Mom's Chicken and Broccoli Casserole (Chicken Divan)

Prep time: 15 minutes │ Cook time: 30 minutes │ Total time: 45 minutes │ Serves: 8

3 to 4 cups fresh broccoli, chopped

5 cups cubed cooked chicken (about 2½ pounds boneless, skinless chicken breast halves)

2 cans cream of chicken soup

1 cup mayonnaise

1 teaspoon lemon juice

½ teaspoon curry powder

½ cup shredded sharp cheddar cheese

½ cup soft bread crumbs

1 tablespoon butter, melted

Preheat oven to 350 degrees F. Grease a 9x13-inch pan.

Bring a large pot of salted water to a boil. Add broccoli and cook 2 to 3 minutes, just until barely tender. Drain off water and arrange broccoli in prepared pan. Place cooked chicken breasts on top of broccoli. In a small bowl, combine soup, mayonnaise, lemon juice, and curry powder; pour over chicken. Sprinkle with grated cheese. Combine bread crumbs with melted butter and sprinkle on top.

Bake 25 to 30 minutes, until crumbs are golden brown and casserole is bubbly.

> **Serving Suggestion:** Add a couple of tablespoons of milk to the soup mixture so that it makes a "gravy" and serve over baked potatoes as a side dish.

Dad's Goulash

Prep time: 5 minutes | Cook time: 30 minutes | Total time: 35 minutes | Serves: 6

1½ pounds ground turkey or ground beef

1 large onion, chopped

1 green bell pepper, chopped

1 (29-ounce) can tomato sauce

2 (15-ounce) cans diced tomatoes, undrained

½ cup brown sugar

1 (15-ounce) can corn, drained

1 teaspoon salt

1 tablespoon Worcestershire sauce

3 tablespoons soy sauce

2 cups dried elbow macaroni

Sauté the ground turkey in a large skillet over medium heat until cooked through. Drain off grease then add onion and green pepper, stirring occasionally until tender, about 5 minutes. Stir in tomato sauce, tomatoes, brown sugar, corn, salt, Worcestershire sauce, and soy sauce.

Let it simmer for about 5 minutes. Add macaroni, stir well, return the lid to the pot and simmer about 20 minutes. When the macaroni is tender, it is done! Serve hot topped with cheese and sour cream.

A Six Sisters' Secret: For a tip on chopping onions, see Cooking Hack #11 on page 149.

Ritz Chicken

Prep time: 10 minutes │ Cook time: 30 minutes │ Total time: 40 minutes │ Serves: 4

4   boneless, skinless chicken breast halves

1   cup crushed Ritz crackers

½   teaspoon garlic salt

Black pepper to taste

2   eggs

½   cup butter

Preheat oven to 375 degrees F.

In a shallow bowl, mix together crackers, garlic salt, and black pepper. In a separate shallow bowl, beat eggs. Dip each chicken breast first in the beaten eggs, and then dredge in the cracker mixture, coating breast completely.

Place coated chicken breasts in a 9x13-inch pan. Cut the butter into small pieces and dot the tops of the chicken breasts.

Bake 30 to 35 minutes, until chicken is cooked through.

Sweet Pork Quesadillas

Prep time: 10 minutes | Cook time: 6 hours 20 minutes | Total time: 6 hours 30 minutes | Serves: 4 to 5

1 (2- to 3-pound) boneless pork butt, shoulder, or loin roast

1 (8-ounce) jar chunky salsa

1 (12-ounce) can Dr Pepper

1 cup brown sugar

10 tortillas

2 to 3 cups shredded Colby Jack cheese

Optional toppings: sour cream, guacamole, pico de gallo, shredded lettuce, salsa, etc.

Put the pork in the slow cooker and fill with water until it reaches halfway up the roast. Cook on high 3 hours.

Drain off the water, cut the pork roast into thirds, and return to slow cooker. In a small bowl, mix together salsa, Dr Pepper, and brown sugar and pour over the pork. Cover and cook on low 3 more hours.

Drain the liquid, reserving 1 cup, and shred the pork. Mix the shredded pork with enough reserved liquid to create a moist, tender mixture; set aside.

Heat a nonstick griddle or skillet to medium heat, place a tortilla on the heated griddle. Sprinkle on about ½ cup cheese and a ½ cup shredded pork and place a second tortilla on top.

Cook 3 to 5 minutes, or until tortilla is golden brown, turning over halfway through. Repeat 3 to 4 more times.

Seven-Can Tortilla Soup

Prep time: 10 minutes │ Cook time: 30 minutes │ Total time: 40 minutes │ Serves: 5

1 (15-ounce) can black beans, drained and rinsed

1 (15-ounce) can pinto beans, drained and rinsed

1 (14.5-ounce) can diced tomatoes, drained

1 (15-ounce) can sweet corn, drained

1 (12.5-ounce) can diced chicken breast, drained, or 2 cooked and shredded chicken breasts

1 (10-ounce) can green chile enchilada sauce

1 (14-ounce) can chicken broth

1 (1-ounce) packet taco seasoning or 2 tablespoons Homemade Taco Seasoning (see recipe on page 103)

1 teaspoon cumin

1 teaspoon chili powder

Add all ingredients to a large stock pot. Bring to a boil, then let simmer on low for 30 minutes. You can also cook this in your slow cooker on low heat for 2 to 3 hours.

Serve topped with shredded cheese, sour cream, diced avocados, and tortilla chips.

> **A Six Sisters' Secret:** To make this a freezer meal, pour all ingredients into a resealable gallon-sized freezer bag. Lay bag flat in the freezer. When ready to use, remove bag from the freezer and place in the fridge. Thaw for 24 hours. Spray slow cooker with nonstick cooking spray. Dump the ingredients from the bag into slow cooker and stir. Cook on low heat for 2 to 3 hours.

The Best Pork Chop Recipe

Prep time: 6 hours 8 minutes | Cook time: 12 minutes | Total time: 6 hours 20 minutes | Serves: 4 to 6

½ cup soy sauce

¼ cup chili sauce

¼ cup honey

2 tablespoons vegetable oil

2 tablespoons finely chopped green onion

1 teaspoon curry powder

1½ pounds boneless pork chops (about 4 to 6 chops)

In a gallon-sized zip-top bag, add the soy sauce, chili sauce, honey, vegetable oil, green onion, and curry powder and mix until completely combined.

Add in the pork chops, then seal the bag. Place in the fridge to marinate 6 to 8 hours or overnight.

Remove bag from fridge, place pork chops on pan or grill over medium-high heat and discard marinade. Grill 6 to 8 minutes on each side or until internal temperature reaches 145 degrees F.

> **A Six Sisters' Secret:** This marinade makes pork juicy and tender. You can also try it with chicken. The flavor is absolutely delicious.

Beef Stroganoff

Prep time: 10 minutes | Cook time: 6 hours | Total time: 6 hours 10 minutes | Serves: 6

1 pound stew meat, cubed

1 (10.5-ounce) can cream of mushroom soup

¼ cup beef broth

½ cup chopped yellow onion

1 (4-ounce) can sliced mushrooms, drained

1 cup sour cream

2 cups cooked noodles

Spray slow cooker with nonstick cooking spray. Combine all ingredients except sour cream and noodles. Cook on low 6 to 8 hours, mixing in sour cream during the last hour of cooking. Serve over noodles.

Slow Cooker Chinese Pork Chops

Prep time: 10 minutes | Cook time: 3 hours | Total time: 3 hours 10 minutes | Serves 6

6 boneless pork chops

1 onion, diced

⅔ cup ketchup

⅓ cup brown sugar

⅓ cup soy sauce

¼ cup water

2 cloves garlic, minced

1½ teaspoons ground ginger

3 cups cooked rice

Sesame seeds (optional)

Sliced green onions (optional)

Spray slow cooker with nonstick cooking spray and add pork chops to the bottom of the slow cooker. Top pork chops with onions. In a medium-sized bowl, mix together ketchup, brown sugar, soy sauce, water, garlic, and ginger and pour over pork chops. Cook on low heat 3 to 4 hours or until meat is fall-apart tender.

Serve over warm rice and top pork chops with sesame seeds and sliced green onions (optional).

Five-Bean Soup

Prep time: 20 minutes | Cook time: 20 minutes | Total time: 40 minutes | Serves: 8

1   green bell pepper, diced

1   onion, diced

2½ teaspoons minced garlic

2   cups vegetable broth

1   (8-ounce) can tomato sauce

1   (15-ounce) can great northern beans, drained and rinsed

1   (15-ounce) can red kidney beans, drained and rinsed

1   (15-ounce) can pinto beans, drained and rinsed

1   (15-ounce) can cannellini beans, drained and rinsed

1   (15-ounce) can black beans, drained and rinsed

2   teaspoons cumin

1   teaspoon paprika

1   teaspoon salt

1   teaspoon garlic powder

½   teaspoon onion powder

½   teaspoon cracked pepper

In a large pot, sauté the bell pepper and onions over medium-high heat until the onions are translucent and flexible. Add garlic and cook and stir 30 seconds. Pour in the broth, tomato sauce, and all the beans. Mix until well combined. Bring the soup to a boil. Add the cumin, paprika, salt, garlic powder, onion powder, and cracked pepper. Mix well until all the ingredients are well combined. Serve with corn chips, green onions, cheese, sour cream, guacamole, or other preferred soup garnishes.

Crispy Coconut Chicken Strips with Piña Colada Dipping Sauce

Prep time: 2 hours 15 minutes | Cook time: 30 minutes | Total time: 2 hours 45 minutes | Serves: 4

- 1 tablespoon hot sauce
- 1 tablespoon fresh lime juice
- ¾ cup canned coconut milk
- 3 boneless, skinless chicken breast halves, cut into strips
- 1 cup bread crumbs
- 1 cup sweetened coconut flakes
- ½ teaspoon salt
- ¾ teaspoon curry powder
- ½ teaspoon onion powder
- ¼ teaspoon pepper
- ½ cup sour cream
- ½ cup crushed pineapple, drained well
- ½ cup piña colada drink mix

Combine hot sauce, lime juice, and coconut milk in a large plastic zip-top bag. Add chicken to the bag and marinate 2 to 3 hours in the refrigerator, turning the bag occasionally so all sides soak in the marinade.

Preheat oven to 400 degrees F. Line a baking sheet with foil and coat with nonstick cooking spray. Combine bread crumbs, coconut flakes, salt, curry powder, onion powder, and pepper in a shallow bowl. Remove chicken from the marinade and roll each strip in the bread crumb mixture. Place on prepared baking and bake 30 minutes or until juices run clear.

Prepare dipping sauce while chicken bakes by combining sour cream, crushed pineapple, and piña colada mix. Serve sauce cold with cooked chicken strips.

Herbed Pork Loin Roast

Prep time: 30 minutes | Cook time: 50 minutes | Total time: 1 hour 20 minutes | Serves: 4 to 5

1 (2- to 3-pound) pork loin roast, with fat left on

1 tablespoon sea salt

2 tablespoons olive oil

2 cloves garlic, minced

1 teaspoon dried thyme

1 teaspoon dried basil

1 teaspoon dried rosemary

Preheat oven to 475 degrees F. Place pork loin in a roasting pan.

Combine remaining ingredients in a small bowl. With your fingers, massage the mixture into the pork loin, covering all the meat and fat. Roast the pork 15 to 20 minutes at 475 degrees, then reduce heat to 350 degrees F. Turn the roast over and roast an additional 35 minutes or until the internal temperature reaches 160 degrees F. Do not overcook or the pork will be very dry.

Allow roast to sit 20 minutes in the pan before slicing and serving.

French Onion Chicken Noodle Casserole

Prep time: 15 minutes | Cook time: 25 minutes | Total time: 40 minutes | Serves: 8 to 10

4 cups diced cooked chicken (about 2 pounds boneless, skinless chicken breast halves)

1 (12-ounce) package egg noodles

2 (14.5-ounce) cans cream of chicken soup

1 (16-ounce) jar French onion dip

1 (10-ounce) can diced tomatoes with green chilies, such as Ro*Tel

1 cup shredded cheddar cheese

1½ cups French fried onions, crushed

Preheat oven to 350 degrees F. Spray a 9x13-inch pan with nonstick cooking spray. Cook egg noodles according to package directions, drain and set aside. In a large mixing bowl, combine chicken, soup, dip, diced tomatoes with green chilies, and cheese. Gently fold in cooked egg noodles and pour into prepared pan. Top with crushed French fried onions and bake 25 to 30 minutes, or until heated through.

Chili Mac Skillet

Prep time: 10 minutes │ Cook time: 35 minutes │ Total time: 45 minutes │ Serves: 6

1 pound ground beef or ground turkey

1 medium onion, diced

1 (15.5-ounce) can pinto beans, drained and rinsed

1 (8-ounce) can tomato sauce

1 (10-ounce) can diced tomatoes with green chilies, such as Ro*Tel

¾ cup uncooked elbow macaroni

⅓ cup water

½ teaspoon garlic salt

1 tablespoon ketchup

1 tablespoon Worcestershire sauce

1 cup shredded cheddar cheese

In a large skillet over medium heat, brown ground beef and diced onions until beef is fully cooked. Drain and return to skillet.

Add in beans, tomato sauce, diced tomatoes with green chilies, uncooked macaroni, water, garlic salt, ketchup, and Worcestershire sauce. Bring contents of pan to a boil and then reduce heat to medium-low. Cover with lid and simmer 20 minutes or until macaroni starts to get tender, stirring often. Sprinkle with cheese, then cover with lid and let cheese melt. Serve and enjoy!

> **A Six Sisters' Secret:** To make cleanup easier, see Cooking Hack # 10 on page 149.

French Dip Crescents

Prep time: 10 minutes | Cook time: 11 minutes | Total time: 21 minutes | Serves: 4 to 6

2 packages refrigerated crescent rolls	Provolone cheese slices
Horseradish sauce (optional)	Easy Au Jus, for dipping (see recipe below)
1 pound deli roast beef, sliced thin	

Preheat oven to 375 degrees F. Unroll crescents onto a large, ungreased cookie sheet.

Spread a small dab of horseradish sauce, if using, on each crescent roll, then place a few slices roast beef and a slice of cheese on each crescent.

Roll up crescents starting from the wide end and ending at the narrow end. Bake 11 to 13 minutes, until crescents are a golden color. Serve with au jus for dipping.

Easy Au Jus

Olive oil	1 tablespoon Worcestershire sauce
¼ cup chopped red onion	2½ cups beef broth
1 teaspoon minced garlic	1 teaspoon flour (optional)
2 tablespoons white wine	

Heat oil in a nonstick skillet over medium heat. Add onions and cook, stirring occasionally, until onions soften and take on a dark, caramel color, about 15 minutes. Add garlic and cook 1 to 2 minutes more.

Deglaze the pot with white wine, then add Worcestershire sauce and cook another minute, stirring constantly. Add beef broth and bring to a light boil. Reduce heat and simmer 30 minutes. Strain broth through a mesh sieve and then return it to pot. Whisk in flour and simmer an additional 5 minutes. Serve with French Dip Crescents.

As you can probably tell, we're huge fans of the slow cooker, and you'll find recipes to put yours to work in nearly every section of this book. This section contains some of our favorites. Taking just a few minutes in the morning to prep a meal leads to huge payoffs at dinnertime when you bring a hot meal to the table after a long and busy day.

SLOW COOKER MEALS

Slow Cooker Honey Garlic Chicken

Prep time: 5 minutes │ Cook time: 6 hours │ Total time: 6 hours 5 minutes │ Serves: 6

4 to 6   boneless, skinless chicken breasts

1   cup light brown sugar

½   cup honey

⅔   cup white distilled vinegar

¼   cup lemon-lime soda

3   tablespoons minced garlic

3   tablespoons soy sauce

1   teaspoon black pepper

2   tablespoons cornstarch

3   cups cooked white rice

Place chicken breasts in slow cooker. In a small bowl, combine remaining ingredients, except cornstarch and rice, and pour over chicken. Cook on low 6 to 8 hours.

Remove chicken from slow cooker and shred in another bowl. Whisk corn starch in liquid in the slow cooker. Add shredded chicken back to the slow cooker and stir well. Serve over cooked rice.

Quick Prep Tip: Use frozen chicken breasts to make this dish even easier.

Serving Suggestion: Garnish this moist and flavorful chicken with chopped green onions and/or sesame seeds.

Slow Cooker Tuscan Soup

Prep time: 10 minutes | Cook time: 5 hours 10 minutes | Total time: 5 hours 20 minutes | Serves: 4

1 medium onion, diced	¼ cup tomato paste
1 large red bell pepper, diced	2 teaspoons minced garlic
2 to 3 boneless, skinless chicken breasts, diced	Salt to taste
	Pepper to taste
1 (15-ounce) can cannellini beans, drained and rinsed	Rosemary to taste
1 (14-ounce) can chicken broth	2 cups fresh baby spinach leaves
	Shredded Parmesan cheese to taste

In the slow cooker, combine the onion, pepper, chicken, beans, broth, tomato paste, garlic, salt, and pepper.

Cook on low 5 hours, stirring occasionally. Add rosemary and spinach and let it simmer an additional 10 to 15 minutes. Serve topped with shredded Parmesan cheese.

> **Serving Suggestion:** Serve with a fresh green salad and a breadstick for a filling, delicious meal.

Slow Cooker Teriyaki Bowl

Prep time: 5 minutes | Cook time: 6 hours | Total time: 6 hours 5 minutes | Serves: 4

2 pounds boneless, skinless chicken breasts

1 cup chicken broth

½ cup teriyaki sauce

⅓ cup brown sugar

3 cloves garlic, minced

2 cups cooked rice

1 cup sliced carrots or whole baby carrots, steamed

1 cup chopped broccoli, steamed

Place chicken in the slow cooker. In a medium bowl, mix together the chicken broth, teriyaki sauce, brown sugar, and garlic. Pour sauce over the chicken and cook on low 6 to 8 hours or on high 4 to 5 hours.

Before serving, steam carrots and broccoli until tender. Add rice and steamed veggies to each bowl. Shred or cut chicken into bite-sized pieces. Add chicken to bowl and drizzle on excess teriyaki sauce from the slow cooker.

A Six Sisters' Secret: This is a great way to sneak a few extra veggies into your kids' mouths. To make it a little healthier, use fat-free chicken broth, low-sodium terriyaki sauce, and brown rice.

Slow Cooker Company Pork Roast

Prep time: 15 minutes | Cook time: 5 hours | Total time: 5 hours 15 minutes | Serves: 6 to 8 servings

2 tablespoons olive oil

1 (3- to 4-pound) pork loin roast

⅓ cup honey

⅓ cup soy sauce

3 tablespoons red wine vinegar

2 teaspoons dry mustard

1 teaspoon salt

1 teaspoon garlic powder

   Pepper to taste

2 tablespoons cornstarch

2 tablespoons cold water

Coat slow cooker with nonstick cooking spray. In a medium skillet, heat olive oil over medium high heat. Sprinkle salt and pepper on roast and then sear all sides of the roast in the olive oil. Place roast in slow cooker (also, scrape whatever is left in the skillet into the slow cooker—it adds good flavor).

In a medium bowl, mix together honey, soy sauce, red wine vinegar, dry mustard, salt, garlic powder, and pepper. Pour over the top of the pork roast and cook on low 5 to 7 hours.

When finished cooking, remove roast from slow cooker and place on a serving platter. Pour remaining liquid from slow cooker into a medium-sized saucepan and heat on stove over medium-high heat. Mix together cornstarch and cold water, then add to saucepan. Cook until sauce starts to thicken, then pour over the top of the pork roast.

Slow Cooker Hawaiian Hula Chicken

Prep time: 10 minutes | Cook time: 4 hours | Total time: 4 hours 10 minutes | Serves: 4

12 strips bacon, cooked but not crisp

4 boneless, skinless chicken breast halves

¼ teaspoon salt

⅛ teaspoon pepper

½ cup chopped red onion

1 (20-ounce) can crushed pineapple, drained

1 cup barbecue sauce

Season each chicken breast with salt and pepper. Then wrap each chicken breast with 2 strips of bacon and place in slow cooker. Top with onion, crushed pineapple, and barbecue sauce.

Cover and cook on low 4 to 5 hours or until chicken is tender. Cook remaining bacon until crisp. Drain and crumble the bacon and sprinkle over each serving.

Slow Cooker King Ranch Chicken

Prep time: 10 minutes │ Cook time: 4 hours │ Total time: 4 hours 10 minutes │ Serves: 8

1 (14-ounce) bag tortilla chips, white or yellow

5 boneless, skinless chicken breast halves, diced

1 (10-ounce) can diced tomatoes with green chiles, drained slightly

1 (10.75-ounce) can cream of chicken soup

1 (10.75-ounce) can cream of mushroom soup

1 cup chicken broth

2 cloves garlic, minced

1 onion, chopped

2 cups shredded cheese

Coat slow cooker with nonstick cooking spray. Spread a layer of tortilla chips in the slow cooker to cover the bottom, followed by half of the diced chicken.

In a medium bowl, combine diced tomatoes, cream of chicken soup, cream of mushroom soup, chicken broth, garlic, and onion. Stir well. Pour half the sauce over the chicken. Top with half of the cheese, followed by the rest of the chips, the remaining chicken, the rest of the sauce, and the remaining 1 cup shredded cheese.

Cook on low 4 hours or high 3 hours. Serve with extra tortilla chips.

Slow Cooker Pork Tacos

Prep time: 10 minutes | Cook time: 8 hours | Total time: 8 hours 10 minutes | Serves 8 to 10

1 (2- to 3-pound) pork shoulder roast

1 (8-ounce) bag dry pinto beans

1 onion, diced

4 cloves garlic, minced

2 (4-ounce) cans diced green chiles

1½ tablespoons chili powder

1½ teaspoons ground cumin

1 tablespoon oregano

1 tablespoon salt

Tortillas

Toppings such as sour cream, lettuce, cheese, etc.

Coat slow cooker with nonstick cooking spray. Place roast inside slow cooker. In a separate bowl, mix together the beans, onion, garlic, green chiles, chili powder, cumin, oregano, and salt. Pour over the roast, then add enough water to the slow cooker so that the roast is almost completely covered. Cook on low heat 8 to 9 hours, checking about half way through to make sure there is still water and adding more water if needed. When roast is done cooking, remove bone and fat and shred pork using two forks. Return pork to the slow cooker and stir into the leftover liquid and serve on tortillas with your favorite toppings.

> **Serving Suggestion:** Use whole wheat tortillas for a healthier option.

Slow Cooker Sirloin Beef Tips and Gravy

Prep time: 10 minutes | Cook time: 7 hours | Total time: 7 hours 10 minutes | Serves: 6 to 8

½	cup all-purpose flour		1	(10.5-ounce) can condensed beef broth
1	teaspoon seasoned salt		2	tablespoons Worcestershire sauce
¼	teaspoon ground pepper		2	tablespoons ketchup
¼	teaspoon garlic powder		2	tablespoons red wine vinegar
3 to 4	pounds sirloin roast tips		2	tablespoons water
2	tablespoons olive oil		½	teaspoon Italian seasoning
1	onion, diced		2	tablespoons cornstarch
1	cup fresh mushrooms		2	tablespoons cold water

Coat slow cooker with nonstick cooking spray. In a medium bowl, mix together flour, salt, pepper, and garlic powder. Dredge meat tips in the flour mixture.

Heat olive oil in large skillet over medium-high heat, then brown tips on all sides. Place beef tips in slow cooker.

Dump onions and mushrooms on top of meat in slow cooker.

Mix broth, Worcestershire, ketchup, red wine vinegar, and water in a bowl. Pour on top of meat in slow cooker. Sprinkle Italian seasoning on top of everything and cook on low 7 to 8 hours.

After meat is finished cooking, mix cornstarch together with water in a separate bowl. Using a strainer, remove beef tips from slow cooker and place in a separate bowl. Pour cornstarch mixture into remaining liquid in the crock pot and mix well. Add the beef tips back into the slow cooker and cook on high for about 10 minutes, until the liquid starts to thicken and turns into a gravy. Serve over hot mashed potatoes.

> **A Six Sisters' Secret:** You can purchase a sirloin roast and cut it into 1- to 2-inch pieces if your store does not carry the tips already. You can also substitute beef stew cubes, which you can find in the meat department of most grocery stores.

Slow Cooker Mongolian Beef

Prep time: 15 minutes | Cook time: 4 hours | Total time: 4 hours 15 minutes | Serves: 6

1½	pounds beef flank steak, cut into strips	¾	cup soy sauce
¼	cup cornstarch	¾	cup water
2	tablespoons olive oil	¾	cup brown sugar
½	teaspoon minced ginger	½	cup shredded carrots
2	cloves garlic, minced	3	medium green onions, chopped

Coat slow cooker with nonstick cooking spray. Place cornstarch in a bowl. Coat each piece of steak in cornstarch and place in slow cooker. Discard any remaining cornstarch. Combine remaining ingredients in a bowl and pour over beef in slow cooker. Cook on high 2 to 3 hours or low 4 to 5 hours. Serve over rice, topped with additional sliced green onions.

Slow Cooker Pork Chops

Prep time: 5 minutes | Cook time: 6 hours | Total time: 6 hours 5 minutes | Serves: 4 servings

- 4 thick-cut pork chops, bone in or boneless
- 1 (10.75-ounce) can cream of chicken soup
- 1 (1-ounce) packet dry ranch dressing mix
- 4 cloves garlic, minced
- ½ cup chicken broth
- Pepper to taste

Combine soup, dressing mix, garlic, and broth. Sprinkle chops with pepper (do not salt). Place chops in slow cooker and pour soup mixture over top. Cover and cook on high 4 hours or low 6 to 7 hours. Serve over rice or mashed potatoes.

Slow Cooker Turkey and Stuffing

Prep time: 15 minutes | Cook time: 4 hours | Total time: 4 hours 15 minutes | Serves: 4

1	pound turkey breast		1	teaspoon poultry seasoning
5	cups herb seasoned dry stuffing		½	teaspoon salt
1	cup sliced fresh mushrooms		¼	teaspoon dried sage
½	onion, finely chopped		¼	teaspoon ground black pepper
2	ribs celery, finely sliced		1	(12-ounce) jar turkey gravy
1	apple, finely diced		1	(10.75-ounce) cream of mushroom soup
¼	cup olive oil			

Spray the inside of slow cooker with nonstick cooking spray and place turkey breast in the bottom of the slow cooker. In a large separate bowl, mix together remaining ingredients. Spread over turkey breast in slow cooker. Cover and cook on low 4 to 6 hours.

> **Serving Suggestion:** Mashed potatoes make a great side dish to this delicious dinner. Especially when served with gravy!

Slow Cooker Gyro

Prep time: 15 minutes | Cook time: 6 hours | Total time: 6 hours 15 minutes | Serves: 6

1   pound boneless, skinless chicken breast halves

3   cloves garlic, minced

¼   cup fresh lemon juice

1   onion, diced

¼   cup water

1   tablespoon olive oil

2   tablespoons red wine vinegar

1   teaspoon oregano

¼   teaspoon allspice

1   teaspoon lemon pepper

Pocketless pita bread

Sliced tomatoes

Sliced onions

Sliced cucumbers

Shredded lettuce

Tzatziki Sauce (see recipe below)

Coat slow cooker with nonstick cooking spray. Place chicken breasts inside slow cooker. In a large bowl, stir together garlic, lemon juice, onion, water, olive oil, vinegar, oregano, allspice, and lemon pepper. Pour over chicken breasts. Cook on high 3 to 4 hours or low 6 to 8 hours. Shred chicken and serve with pocketless pita bread, sliced tomatoes, sliced onions, sliced cucumbers, lettuce, and Tzatziki sauce.

Tzatziki Sauce

2   cucumbers, peeled and seeded

1   (32-ounce) carton plain Greek yogurt

3   cloves garlic, crushed

2   teaspoons red wine vinegar

1   teaspoon lemon juice

½   teaspoon dried dill weed

Salt and pepper to taste

Olive oil

Shred or grate the cucumbers in a food processor or with a box grater. Blot a paper towel or clean kitchen towel to get rid of as much moisture as possible.

In a large bowl, combine shredded cucumbers, Greek yogurt, garlic, vinegar, and lemon juice. Add dill and salt and pepper to taste. Keep in the fridge until serving. This tastes best if you let the flavors come together for at least 30 minutes before serving. Drizzle a little olive oil over the top before serving.

Slow Cooker Chipotle Pulled Pork

Prep time: 10 minutes | Cook time: 8 hours | Total time: 8 hours 10 minutes | Serves: 8 to 10

1 (2- to 3-pound) pork shoulder or butt roast

½ cup ketchup

½ cup brown sugar

½ cup minced yellow onion

1 (8-ounce) jar chipotle sauce

Sandwich buns

Coat a slow cooker with cooking spray. Place the roast in the slow cooker and pour the ketchup, brown sugar, onion, and chipotle sauce on top of it.

Cook 4 to 6 hours on high, or 8 to 10 on low. Remove meat from slow cooker and shred with two forks. Return to the slow cooker, stir, and cook on low until ready to serve.

Slow Cooker Smothered Chicken

Prep time: 15 minutes | Cook time: 4 hours | Total time: 4 hours 15 minutes | Serves: 4 to 6

1 onion, chopped

4 boneless, skinless chicken breast halves

8 slices bacon, cooked and cut into 1-inch pieces

2 cups chicken broth

1 (8-ounce) package cream cheese

4 cups egg noodles, uncooked

2 tablespoons dried parsley

In a large skillet over medium heat, cook onions until they turn soft and golden brown in color.

Place chicken in slow cooker and cover with cooked onions and bacon pieces. Pour chicken broth over top. Cook on low 4 to 5 hours or on high 2 to 3 hours.

About 15 minutes before ready to serve, add cream cheese to the slow cooker. Cook egg noodles as directed on the package. Shred the chicken and mix well to incorporate the cream cheese. Serve chicken over cooked egg noodles and sprinkle with dried parsley.

Slow Cooker Teriyaki Pork Roast

Prep time: 10 minutes | Cook time: 6 hours 5 minutes | Total time: 6 hours 15 minutes | Serves: 6 to 8

1 (2- to 3-pound) pork roast	¼ teaspoon red pepper flakes
½ cup brown sugar, divided	¼ teaspoon black pepper
½ cup chicken broth	½ teaspoon onion powder
½ cup teriyaki sauce	2 tablespoons cornstarch
¼ teaspoon ginger	2 tablespoons cold water
2 cloves garlic, minced	

Coat slow cooker with nonstick cooking spray.

Rub roast with ¼ cup brown sugar and place in slow cooker.

In a bowl, mix together remaining brown sugar, chicken broth, teriyaki sauce, ginger, garlic, pepper flakes, black pepper, and onion powder. Pour on top of roast. Cook on low 6 to 7 hours or high for 3 to 4 hours.

Remove roast from slow cooker and place on plate. Shred with two forks. In a small bowl, mix together cornstarch and cold water, then add to the liquid remaining in the slow cooker. Cook on high 5 to 10 minutes or until it starts to thicken. (To speed up this process, you could pour the remaining liquid in a saucepan and heat on your stove top over high heat until the sauce thickens up.) Pour sauce on top of shredded pork.

Serve over rice or with stir-fried vegetables.

> **A Six Sisters' Secret:** You can also turn this into a freezer meal. Rub roast with half of the brown sugar and place in a gallon-sized zip-top freezer bag. In a bowl, mix together remaining brown sugar, chicken broth, teriyaki sauce, ginger, garlic, pepper flakes, black pepper, and onion powder. Pour on top of roast in bag. Seal bag and place in the freezer. When ready to eat, remove from freezer and place in fridge 12 to 24 hours so that it can thaw. Pour contents of bag in slow cooker and follow the cooking and serving directions above.

Slow Cooker Salsa Verde Chicken

Prep time: 10 minutes | Cook time: 5 hours | Total time: 5 hours 10 minutes | Serves: 6

1½ pounds boneless, skinless chicken breast halves

1 (16-ounce) jar green salsa

1 (14-ounce) can chicken broth

1 medium onion, diced

½ teaspoon cumin

2 cloves garlic, minced

1 (4-ounce) can diced green chiles

Salt and pepper to taste

Coat slow cooker with nonstick cooking spray. Place chicken breasts inside slow cooker. Dump the rest of the ingredients over the chicken and cook on low 5 to 6 hours or high for 3 hours.

Shred the chicken using two forks and incorporate well with liquid in the slow cooker. Serve as filling for tacos, burritos, salad, nachos—anything goes!

A Six Sisters' Secret: To make this a freezer meal, place all ingredients in a gallon-sized zip-top freezer bag. Lay bag flat in the freezer. When ready to use, remove bag from the freezer and place in the refrigerator to thaw overnight. Spray slow cooker with nonstick cooking spray. Dump the contents of the bag into the slow cooker and cook on low 5 to 6 hours or high 3 hours. Shred the chicken using two forks and incorporate well with liquid in the slow cooker.

Freezer meals make life so much easier. A Saturday spent preparing freezer meals means you'll always have something on hand to give your family at the end of a hectic day. Freezer meals are also perfect for welcoming a new family to the neighborhood, delivering to a friend with a new baby, or sharing with anyone in need. Simply drop off the meal with directions for cooking. Add a loaf of crusty bread and a bagged green salad, and you'll have a well-rounded meal. Many of the recipes in this book can be converted to freezer meals by following the same general guidelines in this section.

FREEZER MEALS

Slow Cooker Black Bean and Corn Salsa Chicken

Prep time: 5 minutes | Cook time: 6 hours | Total time: 6 hours 5 minutes | Serves: 4

1 (15-ounce) can black beans, drained and rinsed

1 (14-ounce) can corn, drained

½ (1-ounce) packet taco seasoning or 1 tablespoon Homemade Taco Seasoning

½ cup salsa

⅓ cup water

1 pound boneless, skinless chicken breast halves

Optional toppings: shredded cheese, sour cream, diced avocado, shredded lettuce, diced tomatoes, hot sauce

Label a gallon-sized freezer bag with the recipe name and cooking time.

Dump the black beans, corn, taco seasoning, salsa, and water in the bag and mix until all the ingredients are combined. Add the chicken breasts and zip the bag closed. Place in the freezer until ready to use.

The day before cooking, remove bag from freezer and thaw in refrigerator overnight. Coat slow cooker with nonstick cooking spray. Dump bagged ingredients into the slow cooker, cover, and cook on low 6 to 7 hours or on high 4 to 5 hours.

Shred meat and serve however you want (in tacos or burritos, atop nachos or salads, etc.). Garnish with shredded cheese, sour cream, diced avocado, shredded lettuce, diced tomatoes, and hot sauce.

Homemade Taco Seasoning

1 tablespoon chili powder

¼ teaspoon garlic powder

¼ teaspoon onion powder

¼ teaspoon crushed red pepper flakes

¼ teaspoon dried oregano

½ teaspoon paprika

1½ teaspoons ground cumin

1 teaspoon salt

1 teaspoon black pepper

In a small bowl, mix together all ingredients. Store in an airtight container for up to 3 months.

Slow Cooker Kung Pao Chicken

Prep time: 10 minutes | Cook time: 5 hours | Total time: 5 hours 10 minutes | Serves: 4 to 5

1 pound boneless, skinless chicken breast halves

1 (18.75-ounce) bottle Panda Express Kung Pao sauce

1 red bell pepper, diced

1 green bell pepper, diced

1 bunch green onions, diced

1 (8-ounce) can water chestnuts (optional)

¼ cup chopped unsalted peanuts (optional)

2 cups cooked brown or white rice

Label a gallon-sized freezer bag with the recipe name and cooking time. Place chicken, sauce, peppers, onions, and water chestnuts (and peanuts, if using) in the bag. Zip the bag closed and freeze until ready to use.

The day before cooking, remove bag from freezer and thaw in refrigerator overnight. Coat slow cooker with nonstick cooking spray and dump bagged ingredients into the slow cooker. Cover and cook on low 5 to 6 hours or on high 3 to 4 hours. Remove chicken and cut into bite-sized pieces. Add chicken back to sauce in slow cooker and mix well.

Serve over cooked white or brown rice.

> **Serving Suggestion:** If you prefer crisper vegetables, exclude peppers and onions from the freezer bag. Instead add them an hour before the cooking time ends.

Slow Cooker Country-Style BBQ Spareribs

Prep time: 5 minutes | Cook time: 5 hours | Total time: 5 hours 5 minutes | Serves: 4 to 5

- 1½ to 2 pounds country-style boneless spareribs
- 1½ cups ketchup
- 1½ tablespoons Old Bay Seasoning or seasoned salt
- ½ teaspoon liquid smoke
- ½ cup brown sugar
- ½ cup vinegar

Label a gallon-sized freezer bag with the recipe name and cooking time. Place ribs in bag and set aside. In a medium bowl, combine remaining ingredients and pour over ribs. Zip bag closed and freeze until ready to use.

The day before cooking, remove bag from freezer and thaw in refrigerator overnight. Coat slow cooker with nonstick cooking spray and dump bagged ingredients into the slow cooker. Cover and cook on low 5 to 6 hours or on high 3 to 4 hours.

Slow Cooker Beef and Mushrooms

Prep time: 5 minutes | Cook time: 6 hours | Total time: 6 hours 5 minutes | Serves: 6

3 pounds stew meat, cubed	½ cup apple juice
1 (10.75-ounce) can cream of mushroom soup	1 (1-ounce) packet dry onion soup mix
2 (4-ounce) cans mushrooms, with liquid	3 cups cooked rice or noodles

Label a gallon-sized freezer bag with the recipe name and cooking time. Place stew meat in bag and set aside. In a medium bowl, combine soup, mushrooms, juice, and dry soup mix; pour over meat. Zip bag closed and freeze until ready to use.

The day before cooking, remove bag from freezer and thaw in refrigerator overnight. Coat slow cooker with nonstick cooking spray and dump bagged ingredients into the slow cooker. Cover and cook on high 6 hours or low 10 hours.

Serve over cooked rice or noodles.

Baked Taquitos

Prep time: 20 minutes | Cook time: 30 minutes | Total time: 50 minutes | Serves: 5 to 6

1   tablespoon canola or olive oil

1   medium onion, diced

2   cloves garlic, minced

1   pound lean ground beef

1   (1-ounce) packet taco seasoning or
    2 tablespoons Homemade Taco
    Seasoning (see recipe on page 103)

1   (15-ounce) can black beans, drained
    and rinsed

1   cup chunky salsa

1   cup shredded cheddar cheese

20 (6-inch) flour tortillas
    Nonstick cooking spray
    Salt to taste

Preheat oven to 425 degrees F. Line 2 baking sheets with aluminum foil and spray lightly with nonstick cooking spray.

In a large skillet, heat oil over medium heat. Add onion and garlic and sauté until soft, about 5 minutes. Add beef and taco seasoning, cooking until meat is browned. Add beans and salsa. Mix well and let simmer 5 minutes to allow flavors to meld and the mixture to thicken.

Spoon 2 to 3 tablespoons of the meat mixture into a tortilla, top with a thin layer of shredded cheese, and roll up the tortilla. Place taquitos seam-side down on prepared baking sheets. Repeat. Spray the tops of the taquitos with nonstick cooking spray and sprinkle with salt.

Place pan in oven and bake 15 to 20 minutes, until edges and tops are golden brown. Let taquitos cool completely.

Label 2 gallon-sized zip-top bags with recipe name and cooking time. Transfer cooled taquitos to freezer bags, zip closed, and freeze until ready to use.

When ready to eat, take directly from freezer, remove from zip-top bag, and microwave individual taquitos on high 60 to 90 seconds or until heated through. When reheating multiple taquitos, place on a microwave-safe plate and heat 2 minutes or until heated through. Taquiots can be frozen for about 30 days.

Serve with salsa or your favorite taco toppings.

Slow Cooker Nacho Grande Soup

Prep time: 20 minutes | Cook time: 3 hours | Total time: 3 hours 20 minutes | Serves: 4 to 5

1 pound ground beef

1 medium onion, diced

1 clove garlic, minced

1 (1-ounce) packet taco seasoning or 2 tablespoons Homemade Taco Seasoning (see recipe on page 103)

1 (10.75-ounce) can condensed cheddar cheese soup

1 (10-ounce) can diced tomatoes and green chiles, undrained

1½ cups milk

1 cup shredded cheddar cheese, plus more for serving

Crushed tortilla chips

In a large skillet over medium heat, cook ground beef, onion, and garlic until vegetables are soft and meat is no longer pink; drain off any fat. Stir in taco seasoning, condensed soup, tomatoes, milk, and 1 cup shredded cheese.

Label a gallon-sized freezer bag with the recipe name and cooking time. Transfer mixture to freezer bag, zip the bag closed, and freeze until ready to use.

The day before cooking, remove bag from freezer and thaw in refrigerator overnight. Coat slow cooker with nonstick cooking spray and dump bagged ingredients into the slow cooker. Cover and cook on low 3 to 4 hours. If needed, this soup can be kept on a warm setting for an additional 4 hours.

Stir before serving. Top individual servings with crushed tortilla chips, shredded cheese, and any other toppings you want.

Baked Mac and Cheese

Prep time: 20 minutes | Cook time: 30 minutes | Total time: 50 minutes | Serves: 8

1 (16-ounce) package elbow macaroni, cooked according to package directions and drained well

¾ cup butter, divided

6 tablespoons flour

4½ cups milk

4 cups shredded cheddar cheese

1 teaspoon ground mustard

1 teaspoon salt

Pinch pepper

¾ cup bread crumbs

Grease a 9x13-inch baking dish.

In a large saucepan, melt ½ cup butter over medium heat. Slowly whisk in flour until blended. Cook and stir about 30 seconds and then slowly add in the milk. Bring mixture to a low boil, stirring until it begins to thicken. Remove from heat. Add in cheese, mustard, salt, and pepper, stirring until smooth. Return to heat and add cooked macaroni, stirring until completely combined.

Pour mixture into prepared pan.

Melt the remaining ¼ cup butter and mix it with the bread crumbs in a small bowl; sprinkle buttered crumbs over the macaroni mixture. Cover tightly with several layers of foil and freeze until ready to use.

The day before cooking, remove from freezer and thaw in refrigerator overnight. Preheat oven to 350 degrees F. Remove foil and bake 30 to 40 minutes, or until heated through and lightly browned on top.

Slow Cooker Beef Stew

Prep time: 10 minutes | Cook time: 7 hours | Total time: 7 hours 10 minutes | Serves: 6

1 pound beef stew cubes	2 (10.75-ounce) cans cream of mushroom soup
4 carrots, sliced	
4 to 6 red potatoes, cut into large cubes	1 (8-ounce) can tomato sauce
1 bay leaf	1 (10-ounce) package frozen green peas
1 (1-ounce) packet dry onion soup mix	

Label a gallon-sized freezer bag with the recipe name and cooking time.

Place beef cubes in the bag. Layer carrots, then potatoes, then bay leaf on top.

In a separate bowl, mix remaining ingredients and pour over beef and veggies. Zip bag closed and freeze until ready to use.

The day before cooking, remove from freezer and thaw in refrigerator overnight. Coat slow cooker with nonstick cooking spray. Dump contents of freezer bag in slow cooker, cover, and cook on low 7 to 10 hours or on high 5 to 6 hours.

> **Serving Suggestion:** So yummy with hot bread and honey butter.

Slow Cooker Honey Ribs

Prep time: 5 minutes | Cook time: 6 hours | Total time: 6 hours 5 minutes | Serves: 4 to 6

2	pounds boneless, country-style pork ribs
1	(14.5-ounce) can beef broth
2	tablespoons soy sauce

2	tablespoons pure maple syrup
3	tablespoons honey
3	tablespoons barbecue sauce
½	teaspoon dry mustard

Label a gallon-sized freezer bag with the recipe name and cooking time. Place ribs in the bag and set aside. In a small bowl, combine beef broth, soy sauce, maple syrup, honey, barbecue sauce, and dry mustard. Pour over ribs. Zip the bag closed and freeze until ready to use.

The day before cooking, remove from freezer and thaw in refrigerator overnight. Coat slow cooker with nonstick cooking spray. Dump contents of freezer bag in slow cooker, cover, and cook on low 6 to 8 hours or high 3 to 4 hours.

Slow Cooker Maple and Brown Sugar Pork Tenderloin

Prep time: 15 minutes | Cook time: 7 hours 10 minutes | Total time: 7 hours 35 minutes | Serves: 6

2 (1-pound) pork tenderloins
   Salt and pepper to taste
1 clove garlic, minced
2 tablespoons pure maple syrup
4 tablespoons Dijon mustard
2 tablespoons honey

2 tablespoons brown sugar
1 tablespoon balsamic vinegar
½ teaspoon dried thyme leaves, crumbled
1 tablespoon cornstarch
1 tablespoon cold water

Label a gallon-sized zip-top bag with recipe name and cooking time. Sprinkle tenderloins lightly with salt and pepper and place in bag; set aside.

In a small bowl, combine garlic, syrup, mustard, honey, brown sugar, vinegar, and thyme; pour over the pork. Turn pork to coat thoroughly. Zip bag closed and freeze until ready to use.

The day before cooking, remove from freezer and thaw in refrigerator overnight. Coat slow cooker with nonstick cooking spray. Dump contents of freezer bag in slow cooker, cover, and cook on low 7 to 9 hours or on high 3 to 4 hours.

Remove pork to a plate, cover with foil, and keep warm. Pour the juices from slow cooker into a medium saucepan and bring to a boil over medium heat. Simmer 8 to 10 minutes. In a small bowl, stir together the cornstarch and cold water; whisk into the reduced juices and cook 1 minute longer. Serve pork sliced, with the thickened juices poured on top.

Eggplant Parmesan

Prep time: 30 minutes | Cook time: 35 minutes | Total time: 1 hour 5 minutes | Serves: 4 to 6

2	eggplants, peeled		3	cups spaghetti sauce
	Salt		1	cup Parmesan cheese
3	eggs, beaten		2	cups mozzarella cheese
2	cups Italian seasoned bread crumbs			Fresh basil leaves, chopped

Cut eggplant into ¼-inch thick slices. Layer slices in the bottom of a shallow baking dish, sprinkle with salt, and then cover with water. Let the slices soak for 20 minutes. Drain the water off the eggplant slices and rinse with cold water to remove the salt. Pat dry and set aside on paper towels.

Preheat oven to 450 degrees F. Lightly grease a baking sheet.

Prepare a work station by placing beaten eggs in one shallow bowl and seasoned bread crumbs in a separate shallow bowl. Dip each eggplant slice in eggs, dredge it in bread crumbs, and then place on prepared baking sheet. Bake 5 minutes. Carefully use a spatula to flip over the slices and then bake 5 minutes more. Remove from oven and set aside.

Spread 1 cup of spaghetti sauce in a 9x13-inch pan. Layer with half of the eggplant slices. Add another cup of sauce, spreading it evenly over the eggplant. Top that with ½ cup of shredded Parmesan cheese and 1 cup shredded mozzarella cheese. Repeat with a second layer of eggplant, sauce, and cheeses. Top with basil.

Cover tightly with several layers of foil and freeze until ready to use, up to 1 month.

The day before cooking, remove from freezer and thaw in refrigerator overnight. Preheat oven to 350 degrees F. Remove foil and bake 35 to 40 minutes, or until cheese starts to turn golden brown.

A Six Sisters' Secret: To bake and eat this the same day you prepare it, follow directions above, reducing oven temperature to 350 degrees F. while layering the ingredients in the casserole dish. Bake, uncovered, 30 to 35 minutes.

Ham and Cheese Potatoes

Prep time: 45 minutes | Cook time: 50 minutes | Total time: 1 hour 35 minutes | Serves: 10

2 (10.75-ounce) cans cream of chicken soup

2 cups sour cream

½ cup water

½ teaspoon pepper

2 (28-ounce) packages frozen hash browns, slightly thawed

1 (16-ounce) package Velveeta cheese, cubed

2½ cups cubed cooked ham

Coat 2 disposable 11x7-inch aluminum baking pans with nonstick cooking spray. In a large bowl, mix soup, sour cream, water, and pepper until blended. Stir in potatoes, cheese cubes, and ham. Pour ham and cheese mixture in prepared pans.

Cover pans with foil and freeze until ready to use.

The day before cooking, remove from freezer and thaw in refrigerator overnight. Remove from fridge 30 minutes before baking. Preheat oven to 375 degrees F. and cook, covered, for 40 minutes. Uncover and bake 10 to 15 minutes longer, until thermometer placed in the center of the casserole reaches 165 degrees F.

Bagel Breakfast Sandwiches

Prep time: 10 minutes │ Cook time: 6 minutes │ Total time: 16 minutes │ Serves: 6

6   large eggs, divided

    Salt and pepper to taste

6   bagels, any flavor

6   slices cheese, such as cheddar, Swiss, or provolone

12   slices ham

In a small bowl, beat 1 egg and a pinch salt and pepper with a fork.

Spray a small, microwave-safe bowl—such as a 4- to 6-inch custard dish—with nonstick cooking spray. Pour egg into bowl and microwave 60 seconds (or until cooked through). Remove and set aside. Repeat for remaining 5 eggs.

Split the bagels in half and top 1 half of each bagel with 1 egg, 1 slice cheese, and 2 slices ham. Replace the top of the bagel. Wrap each sandwich tightly in foil and freeze up to 60 days.

The day before serving, remove bagels from freezer and let thaw in refrigerator overnight. Warm thawed sandwiches in microwave on high power in 30-second intervals until you reach desired temperature.

Four-Cheese Lasagna

Prep time: 35 minutes | Cook time: 30 minutes | Total time: 1 hour 5 minutes | Serves: 6 to 8

1   tablespoon salt

1   (16-ounce) package uncooked lasagna noodles

2   (26-ounce) jars spaghetti sauce

1   (16-ounce) container low-fat cottage cheese

1   cup shredded mozzarella cheese

1   cup shredded cheddar cheese

1   cup grated Parmesan cheese

In a large pot over high heat, bring 4 quarts water to a boil. Add salt and noodles and cook 6 to 8 minutes. Noodles should be slightly undercooked. Drain and set aside.

In a blender or with an electric mixer, blend spaghetti sauce and cottage cheese together until smooth. Spoon a little of the sauce mixture in the bottom of a 9x13-inch disposable aluminum baking pan. Place a layer of cooked noodles over the sauce. Sprinkle a portion of the mozzarella, cheddar, and Parmesan cheeses over the noodles. Repeat layers of sauce, noodles, and cheese, finishing with a cheese layer. Cover pan tightly with foil and place in the freezer until ready to use.

The day before serving, remove from freezer and thaw in refrigerator overnight. Remove from fridge 30 minutes before baking. Preheat oven to 375 degrees F. and bake, uncovered, 30 to 45 minutes, or until cheese is bubbly and golden.

Easy Chicken and Noodle Casserole

Prep time: 10 minutes | Cook time: 30 minutes | Total time: 40 minutes | Serves: 6

2 cups shredded cooked chicken (about 1 pound boneless, skinless chicken breast halves)

1 (16-ounce) package egg noodles, prepared according to package directions

1 (10.75-ounce) can cream of chicken soup

1 cup sour cream

¼ cup chopped onion (optional)

½ cup chopped mushrooms (optional)

1 red bell pepper, chopped (optional)

½ cup frozen peas

Garlic salt to taste

Salt and pepper to taste

Coat a 9x13-inch baking dish with nonstick cooking spray. Layer cooked noodles and chicken in the bottom of the dish.

In a medium bowl, combine soup, sour cream, chopped veggies, if using, and frozen peas. Pour mixture over chicken and noodles. Add garlic salt, salt, and pepper to taste and mix well. Cover tightly with several layers of foil and freeze until ready to use.

The day before serving, remove from freezer and thaw in refrigerator overnight. Preheat oven to 350 degrees F. Remove foil and bake 30 minutes, until bubbly and golden brown on top.

Quick Prep Tip: Use a rotisserie chicken from the grocery store to significantly cut down time spent preparing this dish.

Nothing makes cooking more time-consuming than having to wash multiple pots, pans, bowls, and casserole dishes after the evening meal. The recipes in this section cut your dishwashing time significantly. Each one uses only one pot or pan.

ONE PAN, ONE POT MEALS

Easy Baked Salmon

Prep time: 10 minutes | Cook time: 15 minutes | Total time: 25 minutes | Serves: 4

1 (1- to 2-pound) salmon fillet

1 (12-ounce) steam-in-the-bag frozen Brussels sprouts

15 to 20 asparagus spears

2 tablespoons olive oil

Garlic salt

Salt

Pepper

Seafood seasoning

2 tablespoons butter, cut into small pieces

Preheat oven to 400 degrees F. Coat a 9x13-inch pan with cooking spray.

Place the salmon, skin side down, in the middle of the pan. Prepare Brussels sprouts by steaming them in the bag in the microwave according to package directions. Open bag and spread Brussels sprouts on one side of the salmon. Spread raw asparagus on the other side of the salmon.

Drizzle olive oil over both vegetables and sprinkle with garlic salt. Sprinkle salmon with salt, pepper, garlic salt, and seafood seasoning. Dot salmon with butter pieces.

Bake 15 to 20 minutes, or until salmon flakes easily with a fork.

One-Dish Baked Fajitas

Prep time: 15 minutes | Cook time: 45 minutes | Total time: 1 hour | Serves: 6

- 2 pounds boneless, skinless chicken breast halves, cut into strips
- ½ (1-ounce) packet taco seasoning or 1 tablespoon Homemade Taco Seasoning (see recipe on page 103)
- 1 cup salsa
- 1 red bell pepper, sliced
- 1 yellow or green bell pepper, sliced
- ½ onion, sliced
- 2 tablespoons olive oil
  Flour tortillas
  Shredded cheese
  Diced avocado
  Cilantro

Preheat oven to 375 degrees F. Layer chicken on the bottom of a 9x13-inch baking dish. Sprinkle with ½ packet taco seasoning. Pour salsa over the taco seasoning, and then cover with sliced veggies. Drizzle the olive oil over top. Bake 45 minutes, or until chicken is cooked through.

Serve on warm tortillas with cheese, avocado, cilantro, and your other favorite toppings.

Salisbury Steak

Prep time: 10 minutes | Cook time: 30 minutes | Total time: 40 minutes | Serves: 4

1 pound lean ground beef

¼ cup Italian bread crumbs

1 (1.4-ounce) envelope dry French onion soup mix

1 egg, beaten

2 tablespoons water

1 (12-ounce) jar beef gravy

In a large bowl, mix together ground beef, bread crumbs, French onion soup mix, egg, and water. Form the mixture into 4 oval-shaped patties, about ½-inch thick.

Coat a large skillet with nonstick cooking spray and warm up over medium heat. Add the patties to the skillet and cook 10 minutes on each side. Drain the grease from the skillet, and then add in the jar of gravy. Cook steaks in the gravy, covered, for 10 more minutes, flipping halfway through.

One-Pan Chili Beef Pasta

Prep time: 5 minutes | Cook time: 25 minutes | Total time: 30 minutes | Serves: 6 to 8

1 pound ground beef	2 cups tomato juice
3 tablespoons dried minced onion	1½ cups water
1 tablespoon Worcestershire sauce	1 (6-ounce) can tomato paste
2 teaspoons dried oregano	1 tablespoon sugar
2 teaspoons chili powder	8 ounces spiral pasta, uncooked
½ teaspoon garlic powder	3 tomatoes, diced
1 (10.75-ounce) can tomato soup	⅓ cup shredded Parmesan cheese

In a large pot, brown the ground beef over medium-high heat until cooked through. Drain off fat. Stir in dried onion, Worcestershire sauce, oregano, chili powder, and garlic powder.

Add tomato soup, tomato juice, water, tomato paste, and sugar. Stir well, bring to a boil, and let simmer for 2 minutes. Stir in the pasta and reduce heat to medium low. Simmer, covered, 15 to 20 minutes or until the pasta is tender. Stir every few minutes, turning down heat if needed.

Top with diced tomatoes and shredded cheese before serving.

One-Pan Taco Skillet

Prep time: 15 minutes | Cook time: 15 minutes | Total time: 30 minutes | Serves: 8

1¼ pounds ground turkey or beef	1 cup long grain rice
2 green bell peppers, diced	1 cup canned black beans, drained and rinsed
1 onion, diced	1½ teaspoons cumin
2 tomatoes, diced	1 teaspoon garlic powder
1 cup water	1 teaspoon chili powder
1 cup beef stock	1 cup shredded cheddar cheese
½ cup salsa	

In a large skillet over medium heat, begin browning meat. When meat is slightly browned, add diced peppers and onions and cook until meat is completely browned. Stir in tomatoes, water, beef stock, salsa, rice, and beans. Add cumin, garlic powder, and chili powder.

Cover and simmer 15 minutes, or until rice is completely cooked and liquid has been absorbed. Stir in the cheese and top with your favorite taco toppings.

Mushroom Asparagus Chicken Stir-Fry

Prep time: 10 minutes | Cook time: 15 minutes | Total time: 25 minutes | Serves: 4

- 2 tablespoons olive oil, divided
- 2 pounds asparagus, trimmed and cut into 2-inch pieces
- ¾ cup chopped mushrooms
- 3 boneless, skinless chicken breast halves, cut into bite-sized pieces

- ½ cup chicken broth
- 2 tablespoons lemon juice
- 1 teaspoon lemon pepper
  - Pinch fresh cracked pepper

Heat 1 tablespoon oil in a large wok or skillet over medium heat. Add asparagus and mushrooms and sauté 5 minutes, or until asparagus softens. Transfer veggies to a bowl and set aside.

To the hot, empty wok, add remaining olive oil, diced chicken chunks, chicken broth, lemon juice, and lemon pepper. Sauté 15 minutes, or until the chicken is no longer pink and the juices are almost all absorbed. Return veggies to the wok and continue to sauté until the chicken is golden brown and everything is heated through. Add a pinch of fresh cracked pepper before serving.

> **Serving Suggestion:** You can also cook in your other favorite vegetables like carrots, peas, broccoli, or water chestnuts.

One-Pan Italian Pasta

Prep time: 5 minutes | Cook time: 15 minutes | Total time: 20 minutes | Serves: 6

- 2 tablespoons olive oil
- ½ cup diced sweet onion
- 2 to 3 boneless, skinless chicken breast halves, diced
- 1 teaspoon garlic powder
- 12 ounces rotini pasta
- 3 cups water or chicken broth
- 1 envelope dry Italian dressing mix
- 1 cup grape tomatoes, halved
- 1 cup shredded mozzarella cheese
- 1 teaspoon dried basil

Heat oil in a large skillet over medium heat. Add onions and sauté until soft and translucent. Stir in the chicken and garlic powder and cook until browned.

Add pasta, water, dressing mix, and tomatoes. Bring to a boil and cook 10 minutes, stirring occasionally, until water has evaporated. Top with cheese and basil, letting it sit for just a minute so the cheese is melted before serving.

One-Pan Chicken Alfredo

Prep time: 5 minutes | Cook time: 25 minutes | Total time: 30 minutes | Serves: 4

3 tablespoons olive oil	1 cup heavy cream
3 boneless, skinless chicken breast halves, cut into bite-sized pieces	2 cups penne pasta or any bite-sized pasta, uncooked
Salt and pepper to taste	¼ teaspoon dried basil
½ teaspoon Italian seasoning	2 cups grated Parmesan cheese
2 cloves garlic, finely chopped	¾ cup shredded mozzarella cheese
1 (14-ounce) can chicken broth	

Add oil to a large skillet and heat over medium-high heat. Add chicken, season with salt, pepper, and Italian seasoning. Sauté 2 to 3 minutes, or until chicken starts to lightly brown. Stir in garlic and sauté another minute.

Pour in chicken broth, cream, pasta, and basil and stir well. Bring to a boil, cover pan, and reduce heat so mixture simmers. Let simmer 15 to 20 minutes, or until pasta is fully cooked and most of the liquid is absorbed.

Remove from heat and add Parmesan cheese and mozzarella cheese. Stir until cheese is melted and fully mixed in, then serve.

Man-Catching Chicken ⑤

Prep time: 10 minutes | Cook time: 40 minutes | Total time: 50 minutes | Serves: 6

2 pounds boneless, skinless chicken breast halves

½ cup Dijon mustard

¾ cup pure maple syrup

1 tablespoon red wine vinegar

1 teaspoon dried rosemary

Preheat oven to 450 degrees F. Coat a 9x13-inch baking dish with nonstick cooking spray. Layer chicken breasts on the bottom of the pan.

In a small bowl, mix together Dijon mustard, maple syrup, and red wine vinegar. Pour sauce on top of the chicken and sprinkle with dried rosemary. Bake 20 minutes. Flip breasts over and cook another 20 minutes, until chicken is browned and its juices run clear.

Let the chicken rest 5 minutes before serving. Spoon some extra sauce over the top when serving.

One-Pot Creamy Spaghetti and Sausage

Prep time: 10 minutes | Cook time: 14 minutes | Total time: 24 minutes | Serves: 8

2 (24-ounce) jars Ragú Traditional Pasta Sauce

1 (15-ounce) can chicken broth

1 pound thin spaghetti noodles

1 pound precooked Italian sausage, sliced

1 cup cherry tomatoes, halved

1 medium onion, roughly chopped

½ teaspoon garlic powder

½ teaspoon salt

½ teaspoon ground pepper

½ teaspoon Italian seasoning

1 cup water

½ cup sour cream

½ cup shredded mozzarella cheese

Italian parsley, for garnishing

Shredded Parmesan cheese, for garnishing

Pour 1 jar pasta sauce and the can chicken broth into the bottom of a large braising pan or Dutch oven. Break spaghetti noodles in half and toss with sauce and broth. Add sausage, tomatoes, onion, garlic powder, salt, pepper, and Italian seasoning. Pour second jar of spaghetti sauce and 1 cup of water into the pan and turn heat on high. Once mixture starts to boil, reduce heat to medium and cook 9 to 10 minutes, or until the noodles are al dente, stirring frequently.

Reduce heat to low and stir in sour cream and mozzarella cheese. Let it cook over the low heat 2 to 3 minutes, or until the cheese is completely melted.

Scoop into individual serving bowls and top with Italian parsley and shredded Parmesan cheese, if desired.

Sunrise Skillet

Prep time: 5 minutes | Cook time: 25 minutes | Total time: 30 minutes | Serves: 6 to 8

½ pound bacon

4 cups cubed hash browns or peeled and diced potatoes

½ onion, diced

6 eggs, beaten

1 cup shredded cheddar cheese

2 green onions, chopped

Cook bacon in a large skillet over medium heat until slightly crispy; drain on paper towels and reserve 2 tablespoons bacon fat in the skillet.

Add hash browns and diced onions to bacon drippings, cover, and cook until potatoes are tender, about 10 to 12 minutes. Crumble bacon into potatoes. Add beaten eggs and stir until they are fully cooked, about 2 minutes.

Finish by sprinkling with cheese and chopped green onions. Serve immediately.

> **A Six Sisters' Secret:** This simple skillet is all your favorite breakfast foods, deliciously combined into one. It also makes a great breakfast when you're camping, too!

One-Pan Ranch Chicken and Potatoes

Prep time: 10 minutes | Cook time: 35 minutes | Total time: 45 minutes | Serves: 4

8   boneless skinless chicken breasts, halved

5   yellow potatoes, diced

5   large carrots, peeled and chopped

3   cloves garlic, chopped

2   tablespoons olive oil

1   (1-ounce) packet ranch seasoning and salad dressing mix

2   tablespoons chopped fresh parsley

    Salt and pepper to taste

Preheat oven to 375 degrees F. Line a 9x13-inch baking pan with parchment paper.

Arrange chicken, potatoes, carrots, and garlic on the bottom of the pan. Season chicken with salt and pepper. Drizzle olive oil over the top and then sprinkle with ranch seasoning. Toss vegetables and chicken until all are coated in oil and ranch seasoning.

Bake 35 to 40 minutes, or until chicken is cooked through. Cooking time will vary on thickness of chicken and potatoes. For a golden or caramelized look, broil chicken and vegetables 2 to 3 minutes after they are done baking.

Stuffed Pepper Soup

Prep time: 10 minutes | Cook time: 35 minutes | Total time: 45 minutes | Serves: 8 to 10

2 pounds lean ground beef

1 onion, diced

2 cloves garlic, minced

8 cups beef broth

2 (14-ounce) cans diced tomatoes, undrained

2 cups cooked rice

2 green bell peppers, chopped

¼ cup brown sugar

2 teaspoons salt

1 teaspoon pepper

1 tablespoon Worcestershire sauce

In a large stock pot over medium heat, brown beef with onion and garlic until beef is no longer pink. Drain off fat and stir in remaining ingredients. Increase heat to medium high and bring soup to a boil. Reduce heat to low, cover with lid, and simmer 35 to 45 minutes.

Skillet Pizza

Prep time: 15 minutes | Cook time: 30 minutes | Total time: 45 minutes | Serves: 6

1 pound ground Italian sausage

1 medium onion, diced

1 green bell pepper, diced

2 cloves garlic, minced

8 ounces sliced fresh mushrooms

1¼ cups elbow macaroni

1 (14-ounce) jar pasta sauce

1 (14-ounce) jar water

1 (2.5-ounce) can sliced black olives, drained

1 cup shredded mozzarella cheese

1 cup shredded cheddar cheese

15 to 20 slices pepperoni

Grated Parmesan cheese to taste

Salt and pepper to taste

Garlic salt to taste

Heat oven to 400 degrees F.

In large oven-safe skillet, brown sausage, onion, pepper, garlic, and sliced mushrooms over medium-high heat for about 5 minutes, or until meat is cooked through; drain excess fat. Add in macaroni, pasta sauce, water, and olives.

Simmer 15 minutes, or until macaroni is soft and liquid has evaporated. Top with shredded cheese and pepperoni. Sprinkle grated Parmesan, salt, pepper, and garlic salt on top to taste. Bake 15 minutes, until cheese is melted and bubbly.

COOKING HACKS

1. **Wet your fingers** to remove pieces of eggshell from egg white and yolk easily.

2. **If an egg is fresh,** it will sink in water; if it's not, it will float.

3. **Put a few marsh-mallows** in your brown sugar to keep it soft and avoid clumping.

4. **Keep your ice cream** soft and fresh by putting the container in a large zip-top bag.

5. **Remove pomegranate seeds** in seconds by cutting the fruit hor-izontally and placing it seed-side down on your palm. Spread your fingers so the seeds will be able to fall through easily. Hit the top of the pomegranate with a wooden spoon and catch the seeds in a bowl below. They'll come right out!

6. **To get the most juice** out of citrus fruits such as lemons and oranges, microwave them for about 20 seconds and roll them around on a hard surface before squeezing them. You will get almost double the juice!

7. **Softened your butter** too much? Place the too-soft butter in a small bowl. Fill a larger bowl with ice and cold water, then place the little bowl in the ice to let the butter harden a little more.

8. **Place crystallized honey** in a bowl of hot water for about 10 minutes.

9. **Freeze shelled nuts** to preserve their shelf life.

10. **Do you have a pan with sticky residue** that refuses to come off? Fill the pan up with water so all the problem areas are submersed and place on a medium-warm burner on the stove. This can take 10 to 15 minutes, but all the residue will come right off.

11. **Place a piece of bread** in your mouth to keep your eyes from watering when you are chopping an onion. Swim goggles also work for this.

12. **Microwave leftovers** with a separate cup of water alongside them to keep your food moist.

13. **No cupcake or muffin liners?** Cut out parchment paper; it will definitely do the trick.

14. **Measuring sticky ingredients?** Spray the inside of your measuring cups with nonstick cooking spray before filling.

15. **Once a week,** run the dishwasher without any dishes and one cup of vinegar, poured directly in the bottom of the dishwasher. This cleans out any food residue and keeps it smelling fresh.

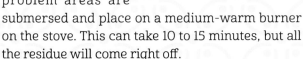

Casseroles are a mainstay in many homes. These are some of our favorites. You'll appreciate how easy they are to throw together and how filling they can be. A good casserole can serve a crowd nicely and is perfect for sharing at potlucks or family gatherings.

CASSEROLES

Creamy Chicken Lasagna

Prep time: 20 minutes | Cook time: 45 minutes | Total time: 1 hour 5 minutes | Serves: 8

- 6 uncooked lasagna noodles
- 1 cube chicken bouillon
- ¼ cup hot water
- 3 cups shredded cooked chicken (about 1½ pounds boneless, skinless chicken breast halves)

- 1 (8-ounce) package cream cheese, softened
- 2 cups shredded mozzarella cheese, divided
- 1 (26-ounce) jar spaghetti sauce
  Italian seasoning to taste

Preheat oven to 350 degrees F.

Bring a large pot of water to a boil. Cook lasagna noodles 8 to 10 minutes, drain, rinse with cold water, and set aside. In a large bowl, dissolve the bouillon cube in the ¼ cup hot water. Add chicken, cream cheese, and 1 cup shredded mozzarella. Stir until well combined.

Spread one third of the spaghetti sauce in the bottom of a 9×13-inch baking dish. Cover with half of the chicken mixture and top with 3 lasagna noodles. Repeat layers. Top with remaining sauce and mozzarella. Sprinkle on Italian seasoning to taste. Bake 45 minutes, until hot and bubbly.

Serving Suggestion: Serve with a dinner roll and a side salad and you have a quick and easy meal!

Cheesy Chicken Quinoa Casserole

Prep time: 45 minutes | Cook time: 25 minutes | Total time: 1 hour 10 minutes | Serves: 6 to 8

1 tablespoon extra-virgin olive oil

1 clove garlic, minced

2 green onions, chopped

1 tomato, chopped

½ cup chopped mushrooms

1 (8-ounce) can tomato sauce

Pinch red pepper flakes

Salt and pepper to taste

Garlic salt to taste

2 cups cooked quinoa

2 cups diced cooked chicken (about 1 pound boneless, skinless chicken breast halves)

½ red bell pepper, chopped

¼ cup chopped cilantro

1½ cups shredded mozzarella cheese

Preheat oven to 350 degrees F. and grease a 9x13-inch glass pan.

In a large skillet over medium-high heat, add olive oil, garlic, mushrooms, and green onions. Sauté 2 to 3 minutes. Add chopped tomato, tomato sauce, red pepper flakes, salt and pepper, and garlic salt. Stir and simmer 5 minutes.

Meanwhile, combine cooked quinoa, chicken, red pepper, cilantro, and ½ cup of the cheese in the prepared pan.

Pour warm sauce on top and mix carefully until everything is combined. Top with remaining 1 cup cheese and cover with foil.

Bake 15 minutes. Remove foil and bake another 10 minutes. Remove from oven and garnish with additional green onions and cilantro, if desired.

Breakfast Sausage Strata

Prep time: 20 minutes | Cook time: 40 minutes | Total time: 1 hour | Serves: 6 to 8

1	pound lean turkey sausage	1	green bell pepper, chopped
12	English muffins, halved	1½	cups sour cream
2	cups shredded cheddar cheese		Salt and pepper to taste
8	large eggs		

Preheat oven to 375 degrees F. Coat a 9x13-inch pan with nonstick cooking spray.

Heat a skillet over medium-high heat. Add sausage and cook until it is browned.

Arrange 6 of the English muffins (12 halves) in the bottom of the pan, cut sides up. Top with half of the sausage and half of the cheese. Place another layer of English muffins and add the rest of the sausage.

In a medium bowl, whisk together eggs, green pepper, sour cream, and salt and pepper to taste. Pour egg mixture over the English muffins so it covers all the bread. Top with remaining cheese and let the dish rest 10 minutes. Cover with foil and bake 40 minutes until cooked through.

> **A Six Sisters' Secret:** You can assemble this the night before. Simply cover and let the eggs soak into the muffins in the refrigerator. For a little spice, add some jalapeño peppers.

Loaded Nacho Casserole

Prep time: 15 minutes | Cook time: 40 minutes | Total time: 55 minutes | Serves: 10 to 12

1   pound lean ground beef

1   large onion, diced

1   green bell pepper, diced

2   (14-ounce) cans diced tomatoes, undrained

1   (15-ounce) can black beans, drained and rinsed

1   (15-ounce) can pinto beans, drained and rinsed

1   (11-ounce) can corn, drained

1   (8-ounce) can tomato sauce

1   (4-ounce) can diced green chiles

1   (1-ounce) packet taco seasoning or 2 tablespoons Homemade Taco Seasoning (see recipe on page 103)

1   (10-ounce) bag tortilla chips

2   cups shredded cheddar cheese

Preheat oven to 350 degrees F. Coat a 9x13-inch baking pan with nonstick cooking spray.

In a large skillet over medium heat, cook the beef, onions, and peppers until meat is no longer pink and vegetables are tender. Stir in the tomatoes, beans, corn, tomato sauce, chiles, and taco seasoning and bring to a boil. Reduce heat to low and let simmer 20 minutes (the mixture will be kind of thin).

Layer half of the tortilla chips in the bottom of the prepare pan, crushing slightly with your hands to make them fit. Top with half of the meat mixture. Repeat layers and then top with shredded cheese.

Bake uncovered 20 to 25 minutes, or until the cheese is melted and the casserole is heated through.

Country Breakfast Casserole

Prep time: 20 minutes | Cook time: 35 minutes | Total time: 55 minutes | Serves: 9

1 pound ground sausage

1 green onion, chopped

2 cups shredded cheddar cheese

6 eggs, lightly beaten

1 cup water

½ cup milk

1 (2.64-ounce) packet country gravy mix

2 cups frozen tater tots

6 slices bread, cubed

2 tablespoons butter, melted

Preheat oven to 325 degrees F. Grease a 9x13-inch pan.

Brown sausage in a large skillet over medium heat; drain off excess fat. Combine sausage and green onion, and transfer to prepared pan. Top with shredded cheese. In a medium bowl, mix together eggs, water, milk, and gravy mix and pour evenly over the pan. Arrange tater tots and bread cubes on top and drizzle melted butter over everything. Bake 35 to 40 minutes.

Cool for 5 minutes, then cut and serve.

A Six Sisters' Secret: This casserole is also great for lunch or dinner.

John Wayne Casserole

Prep time: 20 minutes | Cook time: 30 minutes | Total time: 50 minutes | Serves: 8

2 cups dry biscuit mix

1 cup water

1 tablespoon olive oil

1 green bell pepper, diced

1 onion, diced, divided

2 pounds lean ground beef

1 (1-ounce) packet taco seasoning or 2 tablespoons Homemade Taco Seasoning (see recipe on page 103)

¾ cup water

½ cup sour cream

½ cup light mayonnaise

1 cup shredded cheddar cheese

2 Roma tomatoes, diced

1 (4-ounce) can diced green chiles

Preheat oven to 325 degrees F. Coat a 9x13-inch baking dish with nonstick cooking spray. In a medium bowl, combine biscuit mix and water to make a soft dough. Press dough into the bottom and a half inch up the sides of prepared pan and set aside.

Heat olive oil in a large skillet over medium heat. Sauté the green pepper and half of the onions until crisp-tender. Transfer to a small bowl and set aside.

In the same skillet brown ground beef until no longer pink. Add taco seasoning and ¾ cup water and let simmer 3 to 4 minutes.

In a medium bowl, mix together sour cream, mayonnaise, half of the cheese, and the remaining diced onions and set aside.

Layer the following ingredients, in the order listed, over the biscuit dough in the pan: ground beef, diced tomatoes, sautéed green peppers and onions, green chiles, sour cream mixture, and remaining cheddar cheese.

Bake 30 to 35 minutes or until edges are slightly browned.

Chicken and Broccoli Alfredo Casserole

Prep time: 15 minutes | Cook time: 25 minutes | Total time: 40 minutes | Serves: 8

2½ cups uncooked shell pasta

2 cups broccoli florets, fresh or frozen

4 cups chopped cooked chicken (about 2 pounds boneless, skinless chicken breast halves)

1 (16-ounce) jar Alfredo sauce

¾ cup shredded Parmesan cheese, divided

1½ cups shredded mozzarella cheese

½ teaspoon garlic salt

¼ teaspoon dried basil

Salt and pepper to taste

½ cup Panko bread crumbs

2 tablespoons butter, melted

Preheat oven to 350 degrees F. Coat a 9x13-inch baking dish with nonstick cooking spray.

Prepare pasta as directed on package. Remove from heat, drain water, and dump pasta in a large bowl.

If using fresh broccoli, cut into bite-sized pieces and place in a microwave-safe bowl. Add 2 to 3 tablespoons water and cover the bowl with plastic wrap. Microwave on high power 3 to 4 minutes, or until crisp tender. If using frozen broccoli, prepare according to directions on package. Once cooked, transfer to bowl with pasta.

Add the chicken, Alfredo sauce, ½ cup shredded Parmesan cheese, and mozzarella cheese and stir well. Season with garlic salt, basil, and salt and pepper to taste and spread in prepared pan.

In a small bowl, mix the bread crumbs, melted butter, and remaining ¼ cup Parmesan cheese together. Sprinkle over the top of the casserole.

Bake 25 to 30 minutes, or until the cheese is melted and the edges are bubbling.

White Chicken Enchilada Casserole

Prep time: 15 minutes | Cook time: 30 minutes | Total time: 45 minutes | Serves: 6

4 cups diced cooked chicken (about 2 pounds boneless, skinless chicken breast halves)

1 (10.75-ounce) can cream of chicken soup

2 (4-ounce) cans diced green chiles

1 (16-ounce) carton sour cream

½ onion, finely diced

½ cup milk

½ teaspoon garlic salt

Salt and pepper to taste

1 (10-ounce) bag tortilla chips

1 cup shredded Monteray Jack cheese

1 cup shredded cheddar cheese

Toppings such as shredded lettuce, diced tomatoes, diced avocados, hot sauce, salsa, etc.

Preheat oven to 350 degrees F. Coat a 9x13-inch baking dish with nonstick cooking spray.

In a large bowl, combine chicken, soup, chiles, sour cream, onion, milk, garlic salt, and salt and pepper. Spread chips in the bottom of the baking pan and pour chicken mixture over chips. Top with shredded cheese and bake 30 minutes or until hot and bubbly. Serve with your favorite toppings.

A Six Sisters' Secret: For a tip on reheating leftovers, see Cooking Hack #12 on page 149.

Chicken and Stuffing Bake

Prep time: 15 minutes | Cook time: 40 minutes | Total time: 55 minutes | Serves: 6

6   boneless, skinless chicken breast
    halves

2   (10.75-ounce) cans cream of chicken
    soup

2   teaspoons dried parsley

⅔   cup milk

1   (6-ounce) box Chicken Stove Top
    Stuffing mix, prepared according to
    package directions

    Paprika to taste

Preheat oven to 400 degrees F. Coat a 9x13-inch baking dish with nonstick cooking spray.

Place chicken in prepared pan. In a small bowl, mix together soup, parsley, and milk. Pour on top of chicken. Spread stuffing on top of soup mix and chicken. Cover with foil. Bake 20 minutes. Uncover and bake for 20 to 25 more minutes, until chicken is cooked through. Sprinkle with paprika.

Serving Suggestion: This dish goes well with baked or mashed potatoes topped with the sauce remaining in the pan after baking.

To switch up the dish, add a slice of cheese to each chicken breast before topping with stuffing. Cheddar, swiss, and provolone all taste great with the chicken. Or, mix some sour cream in with the soup before spreading over the chicken.

Poppy Seed Chicken Casserole

Prep time: 20 minutes | Cook time: 30 minutes | Total time: 50 minutes | Serves: 12

2 cups diced cooked chicken (about 1 pound boneless, skinless chicken breast halves)

1 (10.75-ounce) can cream of chicken soup

1½ cups sour cream

1 teaspoon Worcestershire sauce (optional)

1 teaspoon minced garlic (optional)

1 tablespoon lemon juice (optional)

2 cups crushed Ritz crackers

1 tablespoon poppy seeds

½ cup (1 stick) butter, melted

Preheat oven to 350 degrees F. Coat a 9x13-inch baking dish with nonstick cooking spray.

In a large bowl, mix together chicken, soup, and sour cream. Stir in Worcestershire sauce, garlic, and lemon juice, if using. In another bowl, mix together crushed crackers, poppy seeds, and melted butter and stir until butter is completely incorporated.

Spread chicken mixture on the bottom of prepared pan and top with cracker mixture. Cover pan with foil and bake 15 minutes. Remove foil and bake another 15 minutes.

Spinach and Mushroom Pasta Casserole

Prep time: 25 minutes | Cook time: 20 minutes | Total time: 45 minutes | Serves: Serves 8 to 10

- 1 (8-ounce) package uncooked penne pasta
- 2 tablespoons vegetable oil
- 1 cup sliced Portobello mushrooms
- ½ cup (1 stick) butter
- ¼ cup all-purpose flour
- 1 teaspoon minced garlic
- ½ teaspoon dried basil
- 2 cups milk
- 2 cups shredded mozzarella cheese, divided
- 1 (10-ounce) package frozen spinach, thawed and drained
- ¼ cup soy sauce

Preheat oven to 350 degrees F. Lightly grease a 9x13-inch baking dish.

Cook pasta according to package directions until al dente, drain, and set aside.

Heat oil in large saucepan over medium heat. Add mushrooms and sauté 1 minute; transfer to a small bowl and set aside.

Melt butter in the hot saucepan until foamy. Whisk in flour, garlic, and basil to make a roux. Cook and stir 1 minute, and then gradually whisk in milk and stir until thickened and bubbly. Stir in 1 cup shredded cheese until melted. Remove saucepan from heat and stir in cooked pasta, mushrooms, spinach, and soy sauce.

Transfer to prepared baking dish and top with remaining cheese. Bake 20 minutes, or until heated through and cheese is melted.

Fiesta Pork Chop and Rice Bake

Prep time: 15 minutes | Cook time: 1 hour 5 minutes | Total time: 1 hour 20 minutes | Serves: 7

6 to 7 (½-inch thick) boneless pork chops
      Salt and pepper to taste
    2 tablespoons olive oil
    1 (14-ounce) can chicken broth
    1 (8-ounce) can tomato sauce
    1 (4-ounce) can diced green chiles
    1 (1-ounce) packet taco seasoning
      or 2 tablespoons Homemade Taco
      Seasoning (see recipe on page 103)

    1 cup uncooked long grain rice
    ½ cup diced onion
    1 medium green bell pepper, chopped
    1 medium red bell pepper, chopped
    ½ cup shredded Colby Jack cheese

Preheat oven to 350 degrees F. Coat a 9x13-inch baking dish with nonstick cooking spray.

Sprinkle pork chops with salt and pepper. In a large skillet, heat olive oil over medium-high heat and brown pork chops, about 2 to 3 minutes on each side.

In a large bowl, combine chicken broth, tomato sauce, green chiles, taco seasoning, uncooked rice, and onion; mix together until completely incorporated and carefully pour into prepared baking dish. Place pork chops on top of the rice mixture and top with the green and red peppers. Cover with aluminum foil and bake 60 minutes, or until the rice is tender.

Remove from oven, uncover, and top with shredded cheese. Return to oven 5 minutes, or until cheese melts.

Chicken Tetrazzini

Prep time: 30 minutes | Cook time: 50 minutes | Total time: 1 hour 20 minutes | Serves: 10

1 (16-ounce) package linguine

6 tablespoons butter

6 tablespoons flour

½ teaspoon salt

¼ teaspoon pepper

Pinch cayenne pepper

2 (14.5-ounce) cans chicken broth

1 cup half-and-half

4 cups shredded cooked chicken (about 2 pounds boneless, skinless chicken breast halves)

1 cup sliced fresh mushrooms

1 (4-ounce) jar diced pimentos, drained

¼ cup chopped fresh parsley

½ cup grated Parmesan cheese

½ cup shredded mozzarella cheese

Preheat oven to 350 degrees F. Coat a 9x13-inch pan with nonstick cooking spray.

Cook linguine as directed on package. While it cooks, melt butter over medium heat in a large saucepan. When the butter is completely melted, stir in the flour, salt, pepper, and cayenne pepper until mixture is smooth. Carefully pour in the broth, stirring as you pour it in. Bring to a boil and cook 1 to 2 minutes, or until mixture is thickened. Remove from heat and stir in half-and-half.

After pasta is finished cooking, drain, and transfer to a large bowl. Add the chicken, mushrooms, pimentos, and parsley. Pour sauce on top and mix until everything is covered in sauce.

Transfer mixture to prepared pan. Top with Parmesan cheese and mozzarella cheese. Cover with aluminum foil and bake 30 minutes. Remove foil and bake another 20 minutes. Remove from oven and let rest 10 minutes before serving.

A Six Sisters' Secret: This is the perfect way to use Thanksgiving or Christmas dinner leftovers. Simply substitute the cooked chicken for leftover cooked turkey.

Chicken Zucchini Casserole

Prep time: 15 minutes | Cook time: 40 minutes | Total time: 55 minutes | Serves: 6

1 (6-ounce) box dry stuffing mix, such as Stove Top

½ cup (1 stick) butter, melted

4 cups diced zucchini

2 cups cubed cooked chicken (about 1 pound boneless, skinless chicken breast halves)

1 (10.75-ounce) can cream of chicken soup

½ onion, chopped

½ cup sour cream

Preheat oven to 350 degrees F. Coat a 9x13-inch glass pan with nonstick cooking spray.

In a large bowl, combine the stuffing mix and melted butter. Remove and reserve ½ cup of the stuffing mixture for the topping. Add zucchini, chicken, soup, onion, and sour cream to the remaining stuffing in the large bowl and stir well. Spread mixture into prepared pan. Sprinkle reserved ½ cup stuffing mix on top and bake uncovered 40 to 50 minutes, or until golden brown.

> **A Six Sisters' Secret:** This is a delicious way to use up some of the zucchini in your garden. No need to cook it first. For a healthier option, you can substitute ½ cup plain Greek yogurt for the sour cream.

RECIPE INDEX

References to photographs are in *italic*.

CATEGORY INDEX

References to photographs are in *italic*.